Walk with Me Today, Lord

Emilie Barnes

HARVEST HOUSE PUBLISHERS

EUGENE, OREGON

Cover photo © Philippe Devanne / iStockphoto

Cover by Dugan Design Group, Bloomington, Minnesota

WALK WITH ME TODAY, LORD
Copyright © 2008 by Emilie Barnes
Published by Harvest House Publishers
Eugene, Oregon 97402
www.harvesthousepublishers.com

Library of Congress Cataloging-in-Publication Data

Barnes, Emilie.
Walk with me today, Lord / Emilie Barnes.
  p. cm.
ISBN-13: 978-0-7369-2348-4
ISBN-10: 0-7369-2348-9
1. Christian women—Prayers and devotions. I. Title.
BV4527.B363 2008
242'.643—dc22

2008002136

Printed in the United States of America

08 09 10 11 12 13 14 15 16 / VP-NI / 10 9 8 7 6 5 4 3 2 1

To my longtime friend and dear mentor over the years, Florence Littauer. She taught a six-week Bible study in my home with a group of ladies. During those teaching sessions she not only taught God's Word to our group of ladies, but she also inspired me to train to be a teacher and writer about God's Word. I was very fortunate to have her write the foreword for my first book, More Hours in My Day. *At that time in my life I had no idea I had anything to say, but Florence was such an encourager.*

Without her support over the years, I would never have written the many books I have authored. Thank you, Florence, for molding me into the woman I am today.

—EMILIE BARNES

Introduction

Do not merely listen to the word,
and so deceive yourselves. Do what it says.
—James 1:22

God is at work in a mighty way among women in America as well as around the world. More and more women are hearing and responding to His call. Many are naming Jesus as their Lord and Savior for the first time, and others are rededicating themselves to the Lord. If these commitments are to make a significant impact on their families, our nation, and our world, they need to be nourished daily. I pray that this book will help you grow in the Lord.

One way we sustain our commitment to the Lord is by reading His Word daily. The material in this book is designed to challenge and encourage you in your spiritual journey by getting you into God's Word.

In each of the following entries you'll read a passage of Scripture, a short devotional about that passage, a prayer relevant to the message, an action step, and an inspirational thought called Today's Wisdom. With each step you'll be encouraged to embrace and act on what you've learned. James 1:22 challenges us to be not only hearers of God's Word but also doers. We must put God's Word into action.

Don't worry about reading the book from front to back. Skip around if you'd like. On the first page of each entry, you'll find three boxes ☐ ☐ ☐ . Put a checkmark in one of the boxes each time you read the entry. In this way, you can keep track of those devotionals previously read.

May the Lord richly bless you as you listen and respond to His call upon your life.

> God is like a blanket always ready to be wrapped
> 　　around you.
> God is like a chair always there to hold you.
> God is like a pair of arms always ready to wrap
> 　　you in a hug.
> God is like anything you can think of, only
> 　　much better and sweeter.
>
> 　　　　　　　　　　　　—Suzie Godfrew

$\mathscr{M}$ore Than a Mom

One generation shall praise Your works to another,
and shall declare Your mighty acts.
—Psalm 145:4 NASB

$\mathscr{O}$ne of my favorite passages praising the works of the virtuous woman is Proverbs 31:28-31 which reads:

> Her children rise up and bless her;
> her husband also, and he praises her, saying:
> "Many daughters have done nobly, but you excel
>   them all."
> Charm is deceitful and beauty is vain,
> but a woman who fears the LORD, she shall be praised.
> Give her the product of her hands,
> and let her works praise her in the gates (NASB).

When I present my More Hours in My Day seminars around the country, I have the great opportunity to chat with women one-on-one. As we talk, some will tell me, "I'm just a mom," or "I'm just a house-wife." They dismiss their value. I'm always shocked by this and quick to admonish such a low view of their worth. A mother's work is never done; she is a 24/7 worker—always there on a moment's notice. She

7

runs the corporation known as "family," and she controls the foundation known as "home" that makes everybody else's lives comfortable, joyful, and functional.

But do we really see dollar signs when we're serving our loved ones? Hardly! We can't and we don't charge our husbands and children money for loving them. Being a mom and a maker of the home is the greatest calling a woman can have. As the home goes, so goes the world. You play an extremely valuable part in determining the future of our country. There can't be enough praise given to you as a mom. I stand amazed at how much women love their families. Hold your head up high, and know that you are obeying a sacred calling as a mom.

Prayer: Father God, thanks for calling me to be a mom. I ask that You never let me lose sight of who I am in Your eyes. Even if the world doesn't give me honor, I know that You do. Amen.

Action: Take time today to do something just for you.

Today's Wisdom:

> Lord of all pots and pans and things,
> Since I've no time to be
> A saint by doing lovely things
> Or watching late with Thee,
> Or dreaming in the dawnlight
> Or storming heaven's gates,
> Make me a saint by getting meals
> And washing up the plates...
> Thou who didst love to give men food
> In room or by the sea
> Accept this service that I do—
> I do it unto Thee.

—AUTHOR UNKNOWN

ﾑasting Impressions

May my prayer be counted as incense before You;
The lifting up of my hands as the evening offering.
—Psalm 141:2 nasb

Does your body language say "Welcome" to those you come in contact with, or does it say something less warm and friendly, such as "Stay away!"? What people sense in your outward demeanor might be a true reflection of your inner feelings. This is certainly something to think about today! First impressions go a long way in letting people know who you really are.

Our kitchens can tell a lot about our homes as well. Are they spaces that say "Life is happening here!" or do they shout out something less inviting, such as "Disaster Zone! Caution!"? Here are some ideas for creating the kind of kitchen that leaves a lasting good impression on your family and your guests.

- Help a child plant some seeds in a small container and place it in your kitchen window. Watch them sprout.
- Instead of buying commercial applesauce, buy apples and make your own. A bowl of homemade applesauce with a sprinkle of cinnamon is an easy-to-make snack or dessert.

- Stir up a batch of blueberry or cranberry muffins, and bake for a sweet and colorful treat.

- Let your young children experience the satisfaction of boiling eggs, scrambling eggs, and making their own waffles and/or pancakes.

- Teach children how to be organized in the kitchen. "Clean as you go" is a great motto and method.

Make a habit of inviting God to be present at your meals. After the meal is prepared and the table set, pause, hold hands with your family and any guests, and ask the Lord's blessings as you also express thankfulness for the meal and for those gathered around the table. We must not take for granted each meal we eat or the people we love—these gifts all come from above.

Prayer: Father God, thank You for the gift of food. Oh, how we love to eat good food prepared by loving hands. We are grateful that You provide for all our needs. Amen.

Action: Clean out your kitchen cupboards, then reorganize them. Getting your kitchen in order will help make mealtime preparation more enjoyable.

Today's Wisdom:

Perhaps the greatest social service that can be rendered by anybody to this country and to mankind is to bring up a family.

—GEORGE BERNARD SHAW

$\mathscr{W}$hat Good Are Problems?

We can rejoice, too, when we run into problems and trials
for we know that they are good for us—they help us
learn to be patient. And patience develops strength of
character in us and helps us trust God more each time we
use it until finally our hope and faith are strong and steady.
—Romans 5:3-4 tlb

$\mathscr{T}$he problems we face will either defeat us or develop us to be what God wants us to be. We might cry out, "I don't need this problem!" when, in reality, it's just what we need. Unfortunately, most of us fail to see how God wants to use problems for good in our lives. Often we react foolishly and resent our problems rather than pausing to consider what benefit they might bring. Over the years I've learned several basic principles to help me understand why problems exist.

To direct us. Sometimes God must light a fire under us to get us moving. Problems often point us in a new direction and motivate us to change. Is God trying to get your attention? Sometimes it takes a painful situation to make us change our ways. Our family was certainly given new direction when I was diagnosed with cancer. Our family's sense of health and security was initially rocked with that news. Our ministry had launched us into a very busy speaking and writing schedule; our children and grandchildren were doing fine in their lives. Then all of a sudden, *BAM!* The terrible news came that I had to undergo immediate chemotherapy and radiation treatment for a large tumor in my stomach. At that moment, life was changed forever.

As we look back several years later, we see the good in our direction shift. We have met people and experienced events, and I have written five books relating to that time, all of which never would have happened without that problem entering our lives. Problems certainly give new direction to our lives.

To inspect us. Has God ever tested your faith with a problem? What do problems reveal about us? James 1:2-3 expresses the following:

> Dear brothers, is your life full of difficulties and temptations? Then be happy, for when the way is rough, your patience has a chance to grow. So let it grow, and don't try to squirm out of your problems. For when your patience is finally in full bloom, then you will be ready for anything, strong in character, full and complete (TLB).

As an impatient woman, I, too, have been inspected. Hours upon hours of waiting for MRIs, CT scans, blood draws, test results, or direction to start over again after an ineffective procedure have caused me to look deep inside myself to see what I'm made of. Some enlightening has been good, and some has been shocking. I've had to make adjustments when these faults have been exposed. Yes, problems cause you to inspect who you really are.

To correct us. Some lessons we learn only through pain and failures. It's likely that your parents told you as a child not to touch a hot stove. But you probably learned by being burned. Sometimes we only learn the value of something—health, money, a relationship—by losing it.

One of the greatest corrections we faced during that ordeal was to slow down and take time to smell the roses. We had been too busy. God told us to slow down and listen to Him.

To protect us. A problem can be a blessing in disguise if it prevents us from being harmed by something more serious. In our case I'm not privileged to know what we might have experienced because of our situation, but I'm sure of one thing—God had our best under His consideration. He has a master plan and is concerned about every event of our lives. We could sit back and live out one of our favorite theme verses. "And we know that all that happens to us is working for our good if we love God and are fitting into his plans" (Romans 8:28 TLB).

To perfect us. Problems, when responded to correctly, are character builders. God is far more interested in our character than our comfort. Our relationship to God and our character are the only two things we're going to take with us into eternity. Yes, we can rejoice when we run into problems. They help us learn to be patient. God is at work in our lives even when we do not recognize it or understand it. But it's much easier and profitable when we cooperate with God. When we measure success in our lives, we not only measure by our achievements but by lessons learned, lives touched, and moments shared along the way. Our problems have been rich in harvest.

Prayer: Father God, let me have a fuller appreciation of how to handle my problems. Give me the faith, courage, and energy to see the long-term value of my problems. Thanks for caring for me. Amen.

Action: Turn your problems into real learning experiences.

Today's Wisdom:

What you are is God's gift to you; what you do with yourself is your gift to God.

—DANISH PROVERB

You're Wonderfully Made

I will give thanks to You, for I am fearfully
and wonderfully made;
wonderful are Your works,
and my soul knows it very well.
—PSALM 139:14 NASB

In today's verse the psalmist praises God for his unique self, his wonderful existence. Oh, do we ever need people to know that God created them and loves them! At home we have a bright red You Are Special plate that we use constantly. It is brought out for breakfasts, lunches, dinners, birthdays, anniversaries, and various other special occasions. We've served treats on that plate at home, on picnics, at the beach, at the park, in restaurants. You name it, we've done it. There are several things we do extra to reinforce the idea that someone is special:

- We take a photograph of the person with the red plate and put it in a special album just for that special person.

- As we share a meal together with our honored guest, we go around the table, and those present tell why the person is special to them.

- The honored person also gets to share with us why he thinks he is special. Often this person has never thought through why he is special.

Our red plate has become a valuable tradition in our family. We all need to be reminded every once in a while that we truly are fearfully and wonderfully made.

Prayer: Father God, help me realize that because of Your creation I am a very special person. There is no one else quite like me. Thank You for that very special touch—from the very beginning. Amen.

Action: Write down in your journal three things that make you special.

Today's Wisdom:

People travel to wonder at the height of mountains, at the huge waves of the sea, at the long courses of rivers, at the vast compass of the ocean, at the circular motion of the stars; and they pass by themselves without wondering.

—St. Augustine

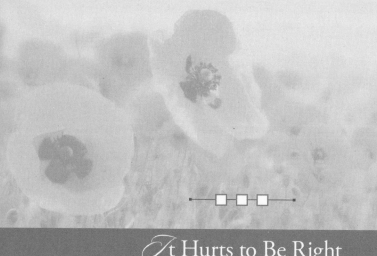

$\mathscr{O}$t Hurts to Be Right

Blessed are those who are persecuted because of righteousness,
for theirs is the kingdom of heaven.
—MATTHEW 5:10

$\mathscr{T}$his verse is taken from Jesus' Sermon on the Mount, a detailed revelation of the righteousness of God and principles that are applicable to the children of God today. These nine beatitudes (blessed means happy) describe the future inner condition of Christ followers.

"Rejoice and be glad, because great is your reward in heaven" (Matthew 5:12). Wow! What a promise. In order to obtain a blessing, there is always a condition. In this case we must be persecuted for the sake of righteousness. It takes a very brave woman to stand up to persecution. The faint of heart need not apply. One prominent Christian once told me, "When I get a lot of criticism, then I know I'm on the right track. Something good is happening." Yes, it truly hurts to be right.

What are these hurts?

- Being persecuted for our different value system.

  "If the world hates you, you know that it has hated Me before it hated you." —John 15:18 NASB

  "All who desire to live godly in Christ Jesus will be persecuted." —2 Timothy 3:12 NASB

"He thought it was better to suffer for the sake of Christ than to own treasures of Egypt, for he was looking ahead to his great reward."—Hebrews 11:26 NLT

- We are ridiculed as moral irritants to the world.

  "They are surprised that you do not run with them into the same excesses of dissipation, and they malign you."—1 Peter 4:4 NASB

- We are an oddity to those around us.

  "If you suffer as a Christian, do not be ashamed, but praise God that you bear that name."—1 Peter 4:16

- Sometimes life just hurts.

  "These things I have spoken to you, so that in Me you may have peace. In the world you have tribulation, but take courage; I have overcome the world."—John 16:33 NASB

- We see red stop signs all through life.

  "The world would love you as one of its own if you belonged to it."—John 15:19 NLT

  "If you want to be a friend of the world, you make yourself an enemy of God." —James 4:4 NLT

What are we to do when it costs to be right?

- Stand firm.

  "Resist [Satan], firm in your faith, knowing that the same experiences of suffering are being accomplished by your brethren who are in the world. After you have suffered for a little while, the God of all grace, who called you to His eternal glory in Christ, will Himself perfect, confirm, strengthen and establish you."—1 Peter 5:9-10 NASB

  "We also exult in our tribulations, knowing that tribulation brings about perseverance; and perseverance, proven character; and proven character, hope; and hope does not disappoint, because the love of God has been poured out within our hearts through the Holy Spirit who was given to us."—Romans 5:3-5 NASB

- Be glad.

"Be very glad—for these trials make you partners with Christ in his suffering."—1 Peter 4:13 NLT

- Follow the example of Jesus.

"[Jesus] was willing to die a shameful death on the cross because of the joy he knew would be his afterwards."—Hebrews 12:2 TLB

Yes, it hurts to be right. Don't think that life's events will always be rosy. There are sufferings to be endured, but, praise God, Scripture has been given to us to give us hope and His promises of our future blessings. Bob and I have realized that we seldom grow during the "good times" of life. It is when we are weak that we become strong. When these sufferings come (as they will), stand firm and be glad, because you know that there is growth just around the corner.

Prayer: Father God, You are a God who knows all about suffering. Your Son, Jesus, was my example as He went to the cross for my sins. Give me the power to stand firm during my times of suffering. Amen.

Action: Turn your suffering into praises. Read James 1:1-4 and Psalm 92:1-4.

Today's Wisdom:

If suffering is accepted and lived through, not fought against and refused, then it is completed and becomes transmuted. It is absorbed, and having accomplished its work, it ceases to exist as suffering, and becomes part of our growing self.

—E. GRAHAM HOWE AND L. LeMESURIER

*G*ive Praises in Everything

Let everything that hath breath praise the LORD.
Praise the LORD!
—Psalm 150:6

We often think that the only way we can praise God is by words or song, but you'll discover that with a little creativity there are endless ways to praise the Lord. I recommend having a welcome sign with a verse of Scripture at your front door to greet your guests. God's praises can be flown as a banner on a pole attached to the outside of your home. There are companies that make flags depicting Christian holidays. This type of praise lets your neighbors and visitors know that you're honoring those specific holidays. They also make good conversation pieces when friends want to know the significance of particular flags.

God can even be honored by the way you decorate your home.

- Who hasn't received a lovely card that just begged to be framed and hung on a wall? There are so many inspirational cards suitable for framing.
- Frame family heirlooms that offer encouragement and are

reminders of the legacy of faith that serves as a foundation for your home today.

- A favorite verse or prayer beautifully showcased in the entry or the guest room will bless anyone who visits your home.

- Hang your family's antique musical instruments or other keepsakes in appropriate places throughout the home. Emphasize the heritage of joy.

- Hang mementos from your children's school days—report cards, certificates of accomplishment, photos, athletic honors, etc. Grown children still love to see these on display.

Did you realize that when you praise the members of your family and give them honor, you are praising and honoring the Lord? After all, it was His idea that you get married, have children, and raise them to be healthy members of our society. Let all of us praise God in our daily lives.

As you make choices in how you decorate your home and express your faith, be sure to explain to your children how these are ways you honor God and show Him praise. They will want to join in the fun, and when they have their own homes and families, they'll carry on the tradition of praising God.

Prayer: Father God, in all that I do, I want to praise You. My creativity is an expression of my praise back to You. You are worthy to be praised. Amen.

Action: Spend an hour in the morning drawing, reading, writing, decorating—indulging your pleasures.

Today's Wisdom:

> Prayer, the basic exercise of the spirit, must be actively practiced in our private lives. The neglected soul of man must be made strong enough to assert

itself once more. For if the power of prayer is again released and used in the lives of common men and women; if the spirit declares its aims clearly and boldly, there is yet hope that our prayers for a better world will be answered.

—ALEXIS CARREL

*C*an You Be Trusted?

I will bow down toward Your holy temple
And give thanks to Your name for Your lovingkindness and Your truth;
For You have magnified Your word according to all Your name.
On the day I called, You answered me;
You made me bold with strength in my soul.
—P<small>SALM</small> 138:2-3 <small>NASB</small>

*A*re there people in your life whom you would trust no matter what they promised you? Are there people who, when they speak, you believe nothing they say? You probably don't have to think very long before names flash before you—in both categories. Unfortunately, we would like to believe everyone, but that's naive on our part. There are some people you don't want to do business with or entrust with your family's needs. You only want truth tellers in your life.

When someone promises me something, I want to know what backs up that promise. Does she have enough financial resources to make that pledge? Does she have the political power to make that promise? Has she been a person of honor who has lived up to her promises in the past?

Our honor is one of our most valuable possessions. It takes years to obtain, but it can be lost in the twinkle of a lie. Your local newspaper is filled with stories about people who have lost their good reputations over a falsehood, a moment of greed, or a bad judgment. As Christians, we need to be people of honor. Do what you say you will do.

God has demonstrated His abiding character and His commitment to keep His promises. When He gives you a promise in His Word, you can take it to the bank. It's sealed with His honor. God's character does not permit Him to break a promise.

As I have walked through my troublesome valley, I can definitely say that God has lived up to every promise. He has heard and answered my prayers. He has been my shield, He has been my protector, and He has given me peace beyond description. He has encouraged me by giving me the strength I needed for the occasion. God can be trusted!

Prayer: Father God, You are honorable in all You say and do. I'm so glad that You are the model for my life. You do what You say You will do. I thank You for all the promises You make and keep. Amen.

Action: Step out in faith today and trust God for the impossible.

Today's Wisdom:

Eternal joy is the end of the ways of God. The message of all religions is that the Kingdom of God is peace and joy. And it is the message of Christianity. But eternal joy is not to be reached by living on the surface. It is rather attained by breaking through the surface, by penetrating the deep things of ourselves, of our world, and of God. The moment in which we reach the last depth of our lives is the moment in which we can experience the joy that has eternity within it, the hope that cannot be destroyed, and the truth on which life and death are built. For in the depth is truth; and in the depth is hope; and in the depth is joy.

—Paul Tillich

*G*rowing Faith in the Garden

Children have never been very good at listening to their
elders, but they have never failed to imitate them.
—James Baldwin

A garden can help people cross boundaries of all kinds. We found our garden to be a sanctuary where we could connect with our grandchildren. All we had to do was invite them to be a part of the whole process, and they were excited to join in the wonder of digging in the dirt without getting in trouble! The time we spent, side by side, working the soil and tending to the plants became our opportunity to act out one of our favorite verses of Scripture:

> These words, which I am commanding you today, shall be on your heart. You shall teach them diligently to your sons and shall talk of them when you sit in your house and when you walk by the way and when you lie down and when you rise up (Deuteronomy 6:6-7 NASB).

We used every opportunity to teach our grandchildren about God and creation. As the children grew, their hands helped till the ground, scatter the seeds, water the plants, prune branches and leaves, and harvest the bounty of flowers, fruits, and vegetables. What child doesn't love to dig in the dirt? What individual doesn't feel that sense of accomplishment when she sees the wonder of the journey from seed to bloom?

Each time the grandchildren visited, they couldn't get out of the van fast enough to see how the plants were growing. Bob often gave them one or more I Was Caught Being Good stickers to show his appreciation for their help. Or he'd take them for a special lunch or dessert at a favorite spot. How close we all became because of those times in the garden! Don't ever underestimate how sharing in the simplest, most basic tasks can become a way of sharing a life and faith together.

Prayer: Father God, let me be sensitive to teach our children and grandchildren in every situation. All situations, good or bad, provide opportunities for learning. Let me never forget this truth. Amen.

Action: Involve your grandchildren in some learning experience. If they live far away, give them a jingle and talk about life.

Today's Wisdom:

We need love's tender lessons taught as only weaknesses can; God hath his small interpreters; the child must teach the man.

—JOHN GREENLEAF WHITTIER

Begin the day with God
   Kneel down to Him in prayer;
   Lift up thy heart to His abode.
   And seek His love to share.
Open the book of God
   And read a portion there;
   That it may hallow all thy thoughts,
   And sweeten all thy care.
Go through the day with God
   Whate'er thy work may be;
   Where'er thou art—at home, abroad,
   He still is near to thee.
Converse in mind with God
   Thy spirit heavenward raise;
   Acknowledge every good bestowed,
   And offer grateful praise.
Conclude the day with God
   Thy sins to Him confess;
   Trust in the Lord's atoning blood,
   And plead His righteousness.
Lie down at night with God
   Who gives His servants sleep;
   And when thou tread'st the vale of death,
   He will thee guard and keep.[1]

You Are More Than a Sparrow

You are worth more than many sparrows.
—LUKE 12:7

In today's secular world, mankind has put equal value on the lives of animals and humans. In fact, many people have more compassion on animals in need than they do on the people around them who are struggling. We don't get it. Genesis 1:26 states: "Then God said, 'Let Us make man in Our image, according to Our likeness; and let them rule over the fish of the sea and over the birds of the sky and over the cattle and over all the earth, and over every creeping thing that creeps on the earth'" (NASB).

Jesus of Nazareth must have been a bird watcher of sorts because He frequently referred to bird life in His sermons:

- "Are not two sparrows sold for a cent? And yet not one of them will fall to the ground apart from your Father."—Matthew 10:29 NASB

- "Look at the birds of the air, that they do not sow, nor reap nor gather into barns, and yet your heavenly Father feeds them. Are you not worth much more than they?"—Matthew 6:26 NASB

- "Indeed, the very hairs of your head are all numbered. Do not

fear; you are more valuable than many sparrows."—Luke 12:7
NASB

One of the great church hymns, "His Eye Is on the Sparrow," written by Civilla D. Martin in 1905, deals with this theme. She gave this account of the writing of this song:

> Early in the spring of 1905, my husband and I were sojourning in Elmira, New York. We contracted a deep friendship for a couple by the name of Mr. and Mrs. Doolittle—true saints of God. Mrs. Doolittle had been bedridden for nigh twenty years. Her husband was an incurable cripple who had to propel himself to and from his business in a wheelchair. Despite their afflictions, they lived happy Christian lives, bringing inspiration and comfort to all who knew them. One day while we were visiting with the Doolittles, my husband commented on their bright hopefulness and asked them for the secret of it. Mrs. Doolittle's reply was simple: "His eye is on the sparrow and I know He watches me." The beauty of this simple expression of boundless faith gripped the hearts and fired the imagination of Dr. Martin and me. The hymn "His Eye Is on the Sparrow" was the outcome of that experience.[2]

What a joy to know that if God watches over the sparrow, He certainly will watch over us who were created in His image. "So God created man in his own image, in the image of God he created him; male and female he created them" (Genesis 1:27).

Over the years Bob and I have adopted Matthew 6:33 as our life's theme verse: "But seek first his kingdom and his righteousness, and all these things will be given to you as well." The phrase "all these things" literally means everything—food, shelter, family, clothing, or your body. Scripture assures us not to worry about these things. Verse 34 follows with: "Therefore do not worry about tomorrow, for tomorrow will worry about itself. Each day has enough trouble of its own."

God is interested in all our cares. If He takes care of the birds of the air, He certainly will take care of our smallest and largest needs.

Prayer: Father God, You are a God who cares for my littlest concerns. Let me always remember the little sparrow when I take things away from You and try to handle them myself. Amen.

Action: Cast your worries on the Lord. This is a faith builder.

Today's Wisdom:

> Why should I feel discouraged?
> Why should the shadows come?
> Why should my heart be lonely
> And long for heaven and home
> When Jesus is my portion?
> My constant friend is He:
> His eye is on the sparrow,
> And I know He watches me;
> His eye is on the sparrow,
> And I know He watches me.

—Civilla Martin

God All Around

May the God of hope fill you with all joy and peace as you trust in him,
so that you may overflow with hope.

—ROMANS 15:13

Do you feel God's presence all around you? When you are struggling, celebrating, making decisions, raising your family, questioning life, declaring faith? During those times, rest in knowing that the God of hope is right there in your journey and is filling you with His hope and peace and joy. When you become aware of God's connection to everything in your life, it becomes easier to talk with Him, trust Him, and seek His wisdom. Read through this inspiring quote:

> Christ ever with me, Christ before me,
> Christ behind me, Christ within me,
> Christ beneath me, Christ above me,
> Christ at my right, Christ at my left,
> Christ in the heart of every man who thinks of me,
> Christ in the mouth of every man who speaks to me,
> Christ in every eye that sees me,
> Christ in every ear that hears me.

—ST. PATRICK

Not only does this quote remind us that God is around us and caring for us, but it is a reminder that God hears, sees, and knows what we do. When we respond to someone out of anger or out of compassion, God hears us. When someone speaks to us in truth and with godly counsel, it is wise for us to pay attention. When we read God's Word and discover His promises, know that they are intended for us. Each and every one.

Prayer: Father God, Help me to believe and embrace the truth that You are all around me. I want to rest in Your love, Your peace, and Your hope. Amen.

Action: Repeat St. Patrick's quote each morning before starting your day. See what a difference it makes in how you approach anything that unfolds.

Today's Wisdom:

> Blessed are those whose strength is in you,
>   who have set their hearts on pilgrimage.
> As they pass through the Valley of Baca,
>   they make it a place of springs;
>   the autumn rains also cover it with pools.
> They go from strength to strength,
>   till each appears before God in Zion....
> For the LORD God is a sun and shield
> the LORD bestows favor and honor;
> no good thing does he withhold
> from those whose walk is blameless.
> O LORD Almighty,
> blessed is the man who trusts in you.
>
> —PSALM 84:5-7,11-12

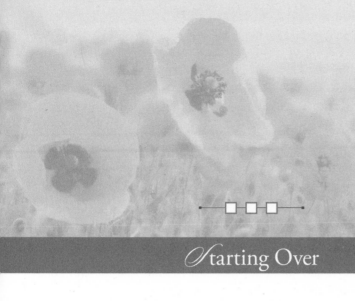

Starting Over

Arriving at one goal is the starting point to another.
—Fyodor Dostoevski

How does one start over? Have you come to a point in life where you have resolved that you need a new beginning? Maybe you've decided that you want to:

- lose some weight and inches
- quit smoking
- lead a healthier lifestyle
- start saving for your children's college education
- pay off your credit-card debts
- be more organized
- live a simpler life

When we've promised ourselves to make a change, it only takes 21 days to form a new habit. But you've got to stick to it. Don't give up. The five tools presented here will reinforce your efforts for change.

Have a plan. I've always said, "If you fail to plan, you plan to fail." It sounds simple, but most of us don't take the time to write down on paper what we'll do to start over. A lot of people want to quit smoking.

So they quit, cold turkey. However, most people can't stop an old habit immediately and begin a new habit right away. It's a lot easier to succeed if we set an overall plan for ourselves to follow.

If your goal is to lose weight or stop smoking, visit your primary-care doctor and let him or her know of your plan. Your doctor can give the support and encouragement you will need along your journey to better health. Simple steps lead to a successful plan.

Set Smarter Goals. We often tend to have high expectations of ourselves, which can lead to very little follow-through. Many times we have other unresolved issues related to areas that we want to change. If it were easy to change, we would have done it a long time ago. In order to achieve big-time goals, we must set bite-size or smaller goals that will bring us closer to achieving our resolution of change.

Smaller and starting goals help you build your strength and stamina to make changes that will lead you to succeed. Each day you are practicing small so you eventually reach your big goal.

Develop a Support System. Find an individual or group of women who will come alongside you to give that all-important encouragement to stick with it. "Don't give up! You can do it!" Words of encouragement give us the proper motivation to keep on going. Announce to your world of family and friends what your goals are, and ask them for support.

Finding a friend who has a similar goal can help tremendously. You can work together and support each other on your journey. All of us will hit the wall at some point in our starting over. Having someone to talk you through it or just listen can be invaluable. You can share information resources and check in on the other's progress. "If two of you agree on earth about anything that they may ask, it shall be done for them by My Father who is in heaven" (Matthew 18:19 NASB).

Don't Expect Perfection. Expect setbacks along the way. No one is perfect, and if you expect perfection of yourself, you will be setting yourself up for failure. Instead, expect improvements from yourself and progress toward reaching your goal. When you do have a setback, get back on the horse and start over again—you will continually be moving forward.

Habits are hard to change. You've spent many years forming the old habits, so don't expect to change them overnight. Be committed to achieving your goal, no matter how long it takes. Don't let yourself get discouraged. Be willing to readjust your timeline as necessary. "Consider it pure joy, my brothers, whenever you face trials of many kinds, because you know that the testing of your faith develops perseverance. Perseverance must finish its work so that you may be mature and complete, not lacking anything" (James 1:2-4).

Give Yourself a Reward. Be proud of your progress; reward yourself on a regular basis. Make a list of things you enjoy doing that can be classified as rewards. Here are some rewards you might consider:

- a new book
- a CD or DVD
- a round of golf or tennis
- go to a sporting event
- get a massage
- take your husband to a play
- join a gym
- take sailing lessons

Make your list personal, and list only those things that give you pleasure. Think positive. Focus on the progress you are making, however small. Keep a "gratitude journal" where you list five things you are grateful for every day.

The more you acknowledge how much you have and are grateful for, the more you will be given.

⚜

Prayer: Father God, help me start over in some areas of my life that need changing. With Your support I know I can do it. It seems like it is such a big effort, but I'm finally at a place in my life where I want to make a change. Amen.

Action: List in your journal the changes you want to make and the things you are going to do to make those changes come about.

Today's Wisdom:

You can't change circumstances, and you can't change other people, but God can change you.

—Evelyn A. Thiessen

Learn to Write on Stone

A friend loves at all times, and a brother is born for adversity.
—Proverbs 17:17

Two friends were walking through the desert. In a specific point of the journey, they had an argument, and one friend slapped the other one in the face.

The one who got slapped was hurt, but without anything to say, he wrote in the sand: "Today, my best friend slapped me in the face."

They kept on walking, until they found an oasis, where they decided to take a bath. The one who got slapped and hurt started drowning, and the other friend saved him. When he recovered from the fright, he wrote on a stone: "Today my best friend saved my life."

The friend who had saved and slapped his best friend asked him, "Why, after I hurt you, you wrote in the sand, and now you write on a stone?"

The other friend, smiling, replied, "When a friend hurts us, we should write it down in the sand where the winds of forgiveness get in charge of erasing it away. When something great happens, we should engrave it in the stone of the memory of the heart, where no wind can erase it."[3]

This story makes me reflect on my own life. How do I write my friends' offenses—in sand or on stone? We need to major on the majors and minor on the minors. Let those minor offenses be written in sand where our memory lets the offenses be forgotten; however, when major events come into our lives, they are to be written in stone where winds never blow them away.

I've been so fortunate in having some great stone friends. They are ones who stand by me during good times and bad times. Yet these friendships took time to develop. Men love to have side-by-side relationships. This is why they bond with men who have like interests: golf, tennis, hiking, fishing, skiing, etc. Most women like friends to be good talkers or ones who can sympathize with their inner emotions and life's journeys.

Having friends is good for one's health and well-being. And being a friend—one who does write of another's kindness and mercy on stone—takes effort, compassion, faith, selflessness, and attention to the hearts and needs of others.

Prayer: Father God, I thank You for giving me such great friends. They enrich my life and give me great happiness. May I be the friend that each one of them needs, and may I always reflect Your heart to the people in my life. Amen.

Action: Go out today and do something for a friend that will be written on stone.

Today's Wisdom:

Promises may get friends, but it is performance that keeps them.

—Owen Feltham

When Jesus Seems Silent

When [Jesus] heard that Lazarus was sick,
he stayed where he was two more days.
—John 11:6

In the eleventh chapter of John, we are introduced to the characters of Lazarus and his two sisters, Mary and Martha. Lazarus was very sick and near to death; Mary and Martha sent word to Jesus to come to them quickly so He could heal Lazarus. They thought Jesus would come immediately, so they were disappointed when Jesus didn't drop everything and come quickly. Instead, Jesus tarried for two days, and by the time He got to them in Bethany, Lazarus had died and was already buried.

Have you ever experienced the silence of God? You have called out, but it's evident, in your eyes, that He isn't there. Why? you ask. Let me share with you two times when Bob and I cried out for healing but God tarried and was silent.

The first time was upon learning of my cancer. We met with the elders of our church for their anointing me with oil. We had never experienced this type of service for ourselves and weren't quite sure what to expect. It was a beautiful and very spiritual experience. We left that event with high expectations. We knew that God was going to heal me immediately. With great anticipation we waited for one day, two days, three days, one week, two weeks, a whole month…and no healing. Why was God silent? We did what the Bible told us to do, but still there were no signs that God was listening.

The second experience came when we went to Seattle, Washington, to the Fred Hutchinson Cancer Research Center for a bone-marrow transplant. They had located a 23-year-old Canadian man who matched my components. We were so excited with very high expectations for healing once again. After being in Seattle for 30 days, I finally was given the donor's bone marrow. Again, we just knew I was going to be immediately healed.

After 85 long days of going to the clinic for blood tests and consultations with the staff, I still wasn't healed. Finally after 125 days we were released to go back home. No healing, but all the blood counts were moving in the right direction. What a day of rejoicing when we got on that airplane to take us back to Southern California.

What did we learn from these two experiences? We began to understand the sound of God's silence. We began to realize that what we wanted wasn't always what God wanted for our lives. *We* wanted immediate results—not healing in two months or two years, but now! We all have agendas, but they are not always God's plans for our lives. God wants us to trust Him more in and with our lives.

Through this searching for what to do when God is silent in our lives, we went back to John 11:4 and adopted this verse as one of our theme verses: "This sickness will not end in death. No, it is for God's glory so that God's Son may be glorified through it." Look also at verses 14-15, "So then he told them plainly, 'Lazarus is dead, and for your sake I am glad I was not there, so that you may believe. But let us go to him.'" Yes, God's timing and purpose are much different from ours. We aren't able to comprehend God's thoughts. But silence doesn't mean inactivity on God's part. He is still there, and His ultimate plan will be revealed in His appointed time.

Charles Spurgeon would often pray: "Lord, don't give me anything that I have prayed for if it's not good for me. Only grant those petitions that are in your plan for my life." This has become our battle cry, because we have come to realize that it's not good for God to give us everything we want.

As Lazarus was ultimately healed (even after he had been in his grave for four days), so was I. It has taken us seven years to get to the quality of life we have. Many times we couldn't see any healing, but God was with us along the way. He was not silent; we just weren't always able to hear Him speaking or discern His leading. We have found that at our most desperate times God is silent, but He has not left or forsaken us. He is always there. We must not confuse God's silence with absence. Not true—He is always with us.

> *Prayer:* Father God, thank You for always being at my side. I so appreciate the assurance that You are with me even when You seem to tarry. Help me to fall in step with Your timing so that I don't turn times of waiting into times of doubt. I want to watch for and rest in Your presence. Amen.

> *Action:* Write in your journal a time when God seemed to be silent in your life. Now jot down what you have learned about God's perfect timing.

Today's Wisdom:

> "Your kingdom come. Your will be done, on earth as it is in heaven."
>
> —Matthew 6:10 NASB

God Is Good

Give thanks to the LORD, for he is good.
His love endures forever.
—Psalm 136:1

Our daughter, Jenny, has a favorite saying, "God is good!" Often she closes a letter or a thank-you note with these three words, "God is good!" From experience in our lives we certainly know that to be true. Even when we have walked though the dark valleys of life, we can praise God for His goodness.

One of the great desires of parents, grandparents, aunts, or uncles is to pass on to those who follow in their footsteps the strengths and wisdom that God has deposited into their lives. I've been working at this for years with my own children and now with my grandchildren. I'm happy to report that in the area of organization, my two children who are grown are more organized than I am. Below are some tips that worked for me. Try them; I'm sure they will work for you too.

Every Sunday evening, review the family calendar together to make sure everyone is on the same page for the week. As you write items on the calendar, color-code the activities for each family member. Yes, I'm serious. Color is something that children understand! Take that idea into all of your home-organizational plans. When our children were little, Jenny knew yellow towels were hers, and Brad knew his were blue. They also had the same colored bins; so when I needed to sort something for Jenny, it went into her yellow bin, and likewise Brad's belongings went into his blue bin.

Every child needs to understand the importance of keeping a tidy bedroom. Our motto was, "If you mess it up, you make it up." Make sure each child has a place to hang clothes and store belongings, and a study center with good lighting for school work, with a bulletin board for special items.

These ideas are not just about keeping your home orderly. These ideas are about making your home peaceful and about providing your children with the skills they need to do the same someday in their own homes and for their own families. The things you do today to encourage your family will be lasting in their lives—that includes living out your faith, creating a sanctuary in the home, and proclaiming "God is good!" no matter the circumstances.

Prayer: Father God, You are good. When I accept Your will for my life, I can relax and be at peace when a new chapter is revealed for me. Every event in my life has a purpose. Amen.

Action: Help your children organize their bedrooms.

Today's Wisdom:

Life is a flame that is always burning itself out, but it catches fire again every time a child is born.

—George Bernard Shaw

Be a Listener

When words are many, sin is not absent,
but he who holds his tongue is wise.
—Proverbs 10:19

I've heard it said that God gave us two ears and only one mouth because He wants us to listen twice as much as we speak. I don't know about you, but I've never had to apologize for something I haven't said. It's much easier and really more natural for us to speak rather than listen. We have to learn to listen. It takes discipline to keep from talking.

As a parent, spouse, sibling, or friend, we need to be known as good listeners. And while listening, we'd do well to remember that there are always two sides to every story. Postpone any judgment until you've heard all the evidence—then wait some more.

Eleanor Roosevelt, in one of her many speeches, stated, "A mature person is one who does not think only in absolutes, who is able to be objective even when deeply stirred emotionally, who has learned that there is both good and bad in all people and in all things, and who walks humbly and deals charitably with the circumstances of life, knowing that in this world no one is all-knowing and therefore all of us need both love and charity."

Our Scripture verse talks to us about being more of a listener than a talker. Too many words can lead to putting one's foot in one's mouth. The more we speak, the greater the chance of being offensive. The wise person will restrain her speech. Listening seldom gets us into trouble, but our mouths certainly cause transgressions.

When others realize that you are a true listener, they will tell you important matters. They will open up about their lives and their dreams. They will entrust you with a bit of themselves and their hearts. Never violate that trust. You have the best model possible in your relationship with God. Without fail, He listens to your every need and hope.

Prayer: Father God, thank You for giving me two good ears to hear. Hold my tongue when I want to lash out. I want to be a better hearer. Amen.

Action: Today, concentrate on listening, not speaking.

Today's Wisdom:

You cannot receive a sincere compliment without feeling better...and just as important; you cannot give a sincere compliment without feeling better yourself!

—Zig Ziglar

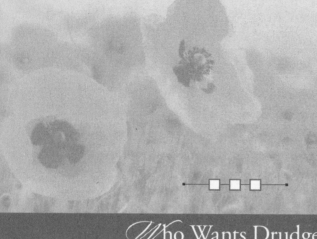

Who Wants Drudgery?

As servants of God we commend ourselves in every way:
in great endurance; in troubles, hardships and distresses; in beatings,
imprisonments and riots; in hard work, sleepless nights and hunger.
—2 Corinthians 6:4-5

Whoever said, "I love drudgery"? Wouldn't it be great if our relationships, careers, and home lives had zero difficulty, trouble, or boredom? Just think how we would greet each day if we only had to do things that were fun, exciting, and pleasing to our personal taste! Our society says, "Only do it if it feels good." Yet, if we did only the feel-good things, we would never have the opportunity to experience those things that develop true Christian character.

Charles Kingsley said, "Thank God every morning when you get up that you have something to do which must be done, whether you like it or not. Being forced to work, and forced to do your best, will breed in you temperance and self-control, diligence and strength of will, cheerfulness and content, and a hundred virtues which the idle never know."

Isn't that a great thought? That as we persevere through our daily living and our life trials, we are gathering virtues right and left. If we rise up and let our lives shine during the doing of drudgery tasks, we can witness transformation that makes drudgery divine.

How do we transform the mundane into the divine? Our Scripture for today (see also verses 6-11) says that as servants of God, we commend ourselves in every way, including:

- great endurance
- troubles
- hardships
- hunger
- purity
- understanding

Paul knew how to take the drudgeries of life and turn them into things divine. In today's language he knew how to turn lemons into lemonade. How can we take all our drudgeries and make them divine? Only when we become servants to one another and let the Holy Spirit strengthen us beyond our human efforts.

In his classic book *My Utmost for His Highest,* Oswald Chambers' devotion for February 19th reads, "Drudgery is one of the finest touchstones of character there is. Drudgery is work that is very far removed from anything to do with the ideal—the utterly mean grubby things; and when we come in contact with them we know instantly whether or not we are spiritually real."

Drudgery must have the inspiration of God in order for us to see it in His proper light. Christ's death on the cross was certainly the greatest form of drudgery, but it was vitally necessary for our salvation. None of our drudgeries will ever be that demanding.

Prayer: Father God, as I look upon the everyday drudgeries of life, may I recognize my commitment to You. May I see the eternal light in these tasks so that I

can recognize that You are building eternal character in my life. Amen.

Action:　Examine two or three of your drudgeries to see
how God can make these into opportunities for
character building.

Today's Wisdom:

When things go wrong, as they sometimes will,
When the road you're trudging seems all uphill,
When the funds are low and the debts are high,
And you want to smile, but you have to sigh,
When care is pressing you down a bit,
Rest, if you must—but don't you quit.

Life is queer with its twists and turns,
As every one of us sometimes learns,
And many a failure turns about
When he might have won had he stuck it out;
Don't give up, though the pace seems slow—
You might succeed with another blow.

Often the goal is nearer than
It seems to a faint and faltering man,
Often the struggler has given up
When he might have captured the victor's cup,
And he learned too late, when the night slipped down,
How close he was to the golden crown.
Success is failure turned inside out—
The silver tint of the clouds of doubt—
And you never can tell how close you are,
It may be near when it seems afar;
So stick to the fight when you're hardest hit—
It's when things seem worst that you must not quit.

—Clinton Howell[4]

Come Clean with God

It is a trustworthy statement, deserving full acceptance,
that Christ Jesus came into the world to save sinners,
among whom I am foremost of all.
—1 Timothy 1:15 NASB

One of the most watched TV series in recent years has been Donald Trump's *The Apprentice*. The highlight of the program is when Mr. Trump delights in saying, "You're fired!" This format has been so well received in America that other networks quickly introduced their versions.

While we never want to hear our bosses utter, "You're fired!" it could happen. But thankfully, we will only hear Jesus say, "You're hired." He gives us new life. But in order for us to be hired, we must humble ourselves and come clean with God. The apostle Paul had the same dilemma when he was challenged to deal with God's grace. Some of these struggles can be found in his writings:

- 1 Corinthians 15:9—I am the least of all the apostles.
- Ephesians 3:8—I am the least deserving Christian there is.
- 1 Timothy 1:15—I am the worst sinner of all.

Paul was humbled by his past and wanted to change his direction in life. At one time in my life I had to make a decision. I had to let old things pass away and then turn to eternal values. As I faced decisions about how I lived and what I wanted, I had to ask, *How do I come close to God?* Examine Paul's challenge in 1 Timothy 2:1-4:

> Here are my directions: Pray much for others; plead for God's mercy upon them; give thanks for all he is going to do for them.
>
> Pray in this way for kings and all others who are in authority over us, or are in places of high responsibility, so that we can live in peace and quietness, spending our time in godly living and thinking much about the Lord. This is good and pleases God our Savior, for he longs for all to be saved (TLB).

Paul gives us three very valuable challenges and instructions: (1) pray for your needs, (2) pray for others, and (3) pray for thanksgiving. Notice that we are instructed to go from our internal needs first and then move to prayers for others and then thanksgiving to God. We are a very narcissistic society. We love to look in the mirror to see how good we look. We are a piece of clay, and He (God) wants to mold us; He doesn't want Madison Avenue doing the job. If we are living lives shaped by the media or by our constant tending to personal, external needs only, then we have to come to a point where we say, "Lord, I need You."

"There is one God and one mediator between God and men, the man Christ Jesus" (1 Timothy 2:5). When we come to a point in life where we want to draw close to God and need direction for our lives, we turn to God and are freed from anger and controversy (verse 8).

Prayer: Father God, help me to come clean. Let me very objectively realize that my present life doesn't fulfill my purpose in life. Give me the courage to realize that I've been wrong in the past and that I want Your salvation for my future. Amen.

Action: Come clean with those you love most—your family.

Today's Wisdom:

We make a living by what we get but we make a life by what we give.

—SIR WINSTON S. CHURCHILL

Easing Your Worries

I tell you, do not worry about your life, what you will eat or drink;
or about your body, what you will wear. Is not life more important than food,
and the body more important than clothes?

—Matthew 6:25

I don't know how things are in your world, but I can tell you that in Southern California we live in an age of anxiety. My neighbors and I have it much easier than our parents, but we certainly are much uneasier than our parents were. We seem to be anxious about temporal things, more so than past generations. They never worried about whether they were eating at the new vogue eatery, vacationing at the best island hotel with the largest pool, wearing the most prestigious label, or keeping their abs in shape.

I watched the previous generation closely; they wanted a home for their families, a car that ran efficiently, and a job that provided for their basic needs. It seems our main concerns and drives today are physical and earth possessed. A large number of people actually believe that if they have the best food, clothing, education, house, and trainer, they have arrived. What else could one want for a perfect life?

Our culture actually places more importance on the body and what we do with it than ever before in modern history. Thus we have created a mind set that causes us as women to be more concerned with life's accommodations along life's journey than with our final destination. Many women are going through their lives with a vast vacuum on the inside. In fact, the woman that you might sometimes envy because of her finely dressed family and newly remodeled kitchen is probably spending most of her day anxious and unsatisfied. Maybe that woman is you?

This thing called life is more important than food, and the body is more important than what we wear. All the tangible distractions don't satisfy the soul; they have become cheap substitutes for our spiritual wholeness and well-being.

Let Christ help you overcome the anxieties of life.

- Stop chasing the temporal things of life. Seek the kingdom of God as it is revealed in Jesus. Cast all your cares on Him.

- Take your eyes off yourself and focus them on God first. Much of our anxieties are rooted in our self-centeredness.

- Spend most of your prayer time praying for others.

- Don't continue to straddle the fence. Commit your total effort and energy to Christ.

The wholeheartedly committed Christian is the truly happy Christian. In Philippians 1:21 we read: "To me, to live is Christ and to die is gain." When we lose sight of who God is and forget to give Him honor, anxiety sets into our lives and day-to-day living doesn't make sense. When we make our goal the pursuit of things and we take our eyes off Jesus, we invariably will be disappointed in our journeys. God does not fail us. He gives us moderation and balance and direction and purpose. A full life.

As I've mentioned, one of our family's favorite verses is Matthew 6:33: "Seek first his kingdom and his righteousness and all these things will be given to you as well." Yes, this is the ultimate anxiety breaker—seek first His kingdom. Bob and I use this as our test for doing anything in life. When we face a decision, we ask ourselves if we are truly seeking His kingdom first, or are we seeking to build our vision of success and value?

In John 16:33 we read: "These things I have spoken to you, so that in Me you may have peace. In the world you have tribulation, but take courage; I have overcome the world" (NASB). God has promised us peace, but many of us choose anxiety instead. We will never be the women God wants us to be until we heed His call—"Come to me, all you who are weary and burdened, and I will give you rest" (Matthew 11:28).

Prayer: Father God, take my eyes off the things of the world. I realize that life is more than things. I know that they don't give my life purpose and meaning. I want to focus on serving You all of my existing days. Give me the power and conviction to follow Your ways. Amen.

Action: Analyze what is making you anxious. What are you going to do about it? Physically write out on a piece of paper what these anxieties are and what you will do to change each into peace.

Today's Wisdom:

Anxiety is the natural result when our hopes are centered in anything short of God and His will for us.

—BILLY GRAHAM

Legacy of Love

In the future, when your children ask you, "What do these stones mean?"
tell them that the flow of the Jordan was cut off
before the ark of the covenant of the LORD.
When it crossed the Jordan, the waters of the Jordan were cut off.
These stones are to be a memorial to the people of Israel forever.
—Joshua 4:6-7

*I*n your family's history there are probably many examples of sacrifice—some you may know about, but many other sacrifices probably took place and were not recorded, mentioned, or elaborated on in family stories and journals. Consider how you have learned life lessons from those who did make sacrifices. What pleasures or luxuries or privileges do you enjoy today because of the toils and trials of past generations? How you honor such sacrifices becomes a part of your legacy to the next generation. If you are raising a family with God's love and truth, that is honoring your life and the lives of those before you. If you are mentoring other women or girls, that is honoring the labor of many women of the past. When you have compassion on a stranger, that is honoring the acts of service that took place before you were born.

We never want to let future generations forget what great sacrifices were made in order for us to be the persons, the families, and the nation we are. That's why traditions are so important in life. They are attempts to pass on to future generations what of value has been passed on to us today.

Joshua built a monument of stones so that the children of the future would ask about them and about their own heritage.

What will your legacy be? What do you hope your children or your friends or your loved ones will carry with them after you are gone? Commit your ways to the ways of God, and your legacy will endure. It will become a heritage of faith and faithfulness that will help to encourage and inspire others. Your legacy won't be in material possessions or in the details of a will. Your legacy will be discovered in the stones…the stepping stones…that created your path—each stone carved and polished by the Creator Himself.

Prayer: Father God, remind me of the sacrifices made by those believers who persevered before me. Remind me of the ultimate sacrifice You made so that my life could be a life of hope and purpose. Amen.

Action: Today, think on the stones you want to gather— commitment, virtue, integrity, joy, service, etc. Build a life upon them so that those who follow will know the story of a life of faith.

Today's Wisdom:

A man is a success who has lived well, laughed often and loved much; who has gained the respect of intelligent men and the love of children; who has filled his niche and accomplished his task; who leaves the world better than he found it, whether by an improved poppy, a perfect poem or a rescued soul; who never lacked appreciation of earth's beauty or failed to express it; who looked for the best in others and gave the best he had.

—ROBERT LOUIS STEVENSON

The Search for Happiness

Blessed is the man
whose quiver is full of [children].
They will not be put to shame
when they contend with their enemies in the gate.

—PSALM 127:5

Storm Jameson, a twentieth-century English writer, wrote, "Happiness comes of the capacity to feel deeply, to enjoy simply, to think freely, to risk life, to be needed." Parents want to make their children happy, employers want to make employees happy, married couples want a happy marriage, etc. "Just make me happy, and I'll be satisfied!" Isn't that what people (ourselves included) think and expect of others a lot of the time? Yet, we run into so many unhappy people—clearly these expectations are rarely met.

Our newspapers are full of stories about unhappy people. They rob, they kill, they steal, they take drugs. They, they, they. Everywhere one looks, there is unhappiness. Then how does one become happy? I've found that happiness comes from one's own perception. No one else is responsible for your happiness. Look in the mirror, and you can see who is responsible for your happiness!

Gerald Brenan wrote:

One road to happiness is to cultivate curiosity about everything. Not only about people but about subjects, not only about the arts but about history and foreign customs. Not only about countries and cities, but about plants and animals. Not only about lichened rocks and curious markings on the bark of trees, but about stars and atoms. Not only about friends but about that strange labyrinth we inhabit which we call ourselves. Then if we do that, we will never suffer a moment's boredom.[5]

Happiness comes from within. It's what you do: the choices you make, the interests you pursue, the attitudes you have, the friends you make, the faith you embrace, and the peace you live. You, you, you bring happiness to your life—no one else. Turn to the One who created you, inside and out, and follow His lead to happiness and wholeness.

Prayer: Father God, sometimes I look for happiness in all the wrong places. I want to have happiness within based on Your love and truth. Thank You for this awareness. Amen.

Action: Begin today to find happiness in your life.

Today's Wisdom:

The strength and happiness of a man consists in finding out the way in which God is going, and going in that way too.

—Henry Ward Beecher

How's Your Attitude?

Gratitude is the attitude that elevates your latitude.

—Dr. Robert Schuller

Attitude plays such a large part in determining our outlook on life. The biggest part of determining our attitude is how much gratitude (or thankfulness) we express along life's journey.

Gratitude + attitude = our latitude in life.

Along life's road we want to deposit a lot of happiness in the bank account of memories, so when we get older, we'll have a plus balance in this account. We withdraw from this account all the time, and if we don't make positive deposits along the way, there isn't anything there to withdraw. Once I received an e-mail that included a sweet story about an elderly woman who was facing the difficult move to a nursing home after her husband had passed away. She was legally blind, and as the attendant described the room that was to be her future home, she immediately said she would love it. When asked how she could know yet, she responded that happiness was something she decided upon in advance! And she had decided she would love the room and find happiness in each day she lived.

This story certainly inspires an important point—our joy is not determined as situations and trials and celebrations unfold but by our attitude going into life, day by day. Not only does this approach accumulate happiness after happiness in our memory accounts, but this attitude leads us toward a life that notices and embraces God's goodness.

If your tendency is to subtract from your joy reserves by facing days with grumbling or doubt or regret, turn your attitude toward gratitude—and the view along your journey will be much more vibrant, alive, and filled with God's hope.

Prayer: Father God, help me formulate a formula for life. I want to be a happy person. One with a good attitude. Let those around me be lifted up by my positive attitude. Amen.

Action: Deposit a lot of happiness in your bank account of memories.

Today's Wisdom:

Be careful for nothing, prayerful for everything, thankful for anything.

—Dwight L. Moody

Children Are a Gift

Behold, children are a gift of the LORD;
the fruit of the womb is a reward.
Like arrows in the hand of a warrior,
so are the children of one's youth.

—Psalm 127:3 NASB

In a recent women's Bible study, the teacher asked the group, "Did you feel loved by your parents when you were a child?" Here are some of the responses.

- "A lot of pizza came to the house on Friday nights when my parents went out for the evening."
- "I got in their way. I wasn't important to them."
- "They were too busy for me."
- "Mom didn't have to work, but she did just so she wouldn't have to be home with us kids."
- "I spent too much time with a babysitter."
- "Mom was too involved at the country club to spend time with me."

- "Dad took us on trips, but he played golf all the time we were away."

So many of the ladies felt they were rejected by their parents in their childhoods. There was very little love in their homes. What would your children say in response to the same question? I'm sure we all would gain insight from our children's answers.

In today's verse we see that children are a reward (gift) from the Lord. In Hebrew, "gift" means "property—a possession." Truly, God has loaned us His property or possessions to care for and to enjoy for a certain period of time.

My Bob loves to grow vegetables in his raised-bed garden each summer. I am amazed at what it takes to get a good crop. He cultivates the soil, sows seeds, waters, fertilizes, weeds, and prunes. Raising children takes a lot of time, care, nurturing, and cultivating as well. We can't neglect these responsibilities if we are going to produce good fruit. Left to itself, the garden—and our children—will end up weeds.

Bob always has a smile on his face when he brings a big basket full of corn, tomatoes, cucumbers, and beans into the kitchen. As the harvest is Bob's reward, so children are parents' rewards.

Let your home be a place where its members come to be rejuvenated after a very busy time away from it. We liked to call our home the "trauma center"—a place where we could make mistakes, but also where there was healing. Perfect people didn't reside at our address. We tried to teach that we all make mistakes and certainly aren't always right. Quite often in our home we could hear the two most important words, "I'm sorry."

Prayer: Father God, thank You for giving me the joy of family. Help me to create a place where there is forgiveness and love. My children are truly a reward for me, and they come straight from You. Thank You. Amen.

Action: Be bold and ask your children tonight, "Do you feel loved in our home?" Be ready for unexpected answers.

Today's Wisdom:

Discipline is demanded of the athlete to win a game. Discipline is required for the captain running his ship. Discipline is needed for the pianist to practice for the concert. Only in the matter of personal conduct is the need for discipline questioned. But if parents believe standards are necessary, then discipline is needed to attain them.

—GLADYS BROOKS

Being a Helper

It is not good for the man to be alone.
I will make a helper suitable for him.
—Genesis 2:18

One of the joys of being an older woman is helping teach the younger women how to be helpers for their husbands. Daughters and daughters-in-law need to hear your wisdom when it comes to marriage. Sharing your experience becomes a great reward of your station in life. When I make this suggestion to a group, many women who have adult children will quietly comment that they don't have anything to teach anyone else. In fact, they are intimidated by the next generation and feel insecure about their experience. This is the perfect reason to begin mentoring another woman. You'll both discover the depth and breadth of your wisdom as wives and mothers.

As a mature adult, you can be the one who encourages your daughters and daughters-in-law in how to be helpers to their mates, one of the great principles of marriage. What a difference it would make if more women would uphold their husbands as they attempt to rise above the pull of the world and toward God's purposes.

You can be the facilitator who will help women to understand and implement Paul's teaching in Titus 2:3-5: "Teach the older women to be reverent in the way they live.... Then they can train the younger women to love their husbands and children, to be self-controlled and pure, to be busy at home, to be kind, and to be subject to their husbands, so that no one will malign the word of God."

As a grandparent, the easiest way to teach is by example. Often married children are not eager to ask their parents about marriage, but they cannot deny your living and modeling Scripture. Be available to help when it is requested. We must be sensitive that we don't barge unannounced into their lives, but be prepared when the time comes.

Prayer: Father God, as a mature woman of God, I want to be used to encourage other women how to be makers of their homes. Give me the perfect timing to be available. In the meantime I will demonstrate Your Word by my life. Amen.

Action: Tell your husband how much you love him.

Today's Wisdom:

Eternity is not something that begins after you are dead. It is going on all the time. We are in it now.

—CHARLOTTE PERKINS GILMAN

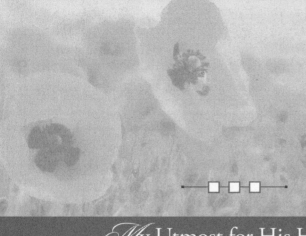

My Utmost for His Highest

*If you then, though you are evil, know how to give good gifts
to your children, how much more will your Father in heaven give
the Holy Spirit to those who ask him!*
—Luke 11:13

This verse had a huge impact on the life of the great twentieth-century Christian preacher, teacher, and writer Oswald Chambers. After surrendering his life to Christ under the teaching of Charles Spurgeon, and even after entering the ministry, he claimed he was dry and empty, having no power or strong realization of God. After years of searching for more authority and power of presentation for his writing and speaking, Oswald claimed the promise of Luke 11:13. He said, "Like a flash something happened inside me, and I saw that I had been wanting power in my own hand.... The power and the tyranny of sin is gone and the radiant, unspeakable emancipation of the indwelling Christ has come." From that day on he found power and peace in ministry that impacted the world both during and after his life.

He died suddenly in Egypt on November 15, 1917, while serving British troops during World War I and was buried in Cairo under a headstone bearing the words of Luke 11:13. Only later did his widow, Gertrude Hobbs Chambers, compile his manuscripts, notes, lectures, and sermons into *My Utmost for His Highest,* a classic book that is read by Christians all over the world.

Charles C. Ryrie, in his New American Standard *Ryrie Study Bible,* makes this comment in his footnotes on Luke 11:13: "Since the day of Pentecost the gift of the Spirit is given to all believers."[7] In Acts 10:44 we read that the Holy Spirit fell upon all those who were listening to Peter's message. And in verse 45 we read where both the Jews and Gentiles received this power.

Maybe you find yourself dried out, burned out, and with no power in your Christian walk. You search your heart and want to know where that first love has gone. Yes, we all can be living powerless lives as Oswald Chambers was until he was touched by Luke 11:13. If this is where you are, claim the promise of God that as believers we have the power and might of the third person of the Trinity—the Holy Spirit. Study more on who the Holy Spirit is, and ask God to grant you all the privileges that go with this knowledge.

Prayer: Father God, I come to You, not experiencing this power of ministry that Oswald had. Awaken my soul that I might claim what has already been given to me. I want to exhibit power in my beliefs and live by Your strength. Amen.

Action: Claim all the provisions given by possessing the Holy Spirit in your life.

Today's Wisdom:

Without the presence of the Spirit there is no conviction, no regeneration, no sanctification, no cleansing, no acceptable works. We can perform duties without Him, but our service is dull and mechanical. Life is in the quickening Spirit.

—W. A. CRISWELL

*D*on't Run on Emptiness

Elijah was a man with a nature like ours.
—JAMES 5:17 NASB

*H*ave you ever been to a large concert or a speaking event with thousands of others around you talking or clapping or singing and still felt alone or empty? That feeling is very common to those of us who are living in a merry-go-round world. So much noise, but so little caring. Elijah of the Bible felt just like that—empty with no purpose in life. In 1 Kings 19:1-18 we find him:

- v. 2—being threatened to have his life taken;
- v. 3—afraid;
- v. 4—praying that he might die;
- v. 5—touched by an angel who said, "Arise, eat.";
- v. 9—asked by the Lord, "What are you doing here?";
- v. 11—being told to go stand on the mountain before the LORD;
- vv. 11-12—confronted by strong winds, an earthquake, a fire, and a sound of gentle blowing (or a gentle whisper);

- v. 14—telling the LORD he had done all the LORD had asked and that he alone was left.

Yes, Elijah was as human as we are. He was threatened, he was alone, he wanted to die, he was confused, he wanted to give in and call it quits. But he didn't, he went on top of the mountain. In verses 11-12 he heard the sound of a gentle whisper. He could have ignored the message, but he didn't. By wise counsel from the Lord, Elijah was assured that he wasn't done (vv. 15-16); he wasn't alone (v. 16); he wasn't a failure (v. 18).

If you find yourself in that empty state like Elijah, you, too, can be assured that you are not done, not alone, and not a failure. Listen to that gentle whisper and get back on track. How does one get back on the right track? Scripture gives us four ways to get away so we can hear the whisper of God's voice:

1. Go to a quiet spot.

   "Very early in the morning, while it was still dark, Jesus got up, left the house and went off to a solitary place, where he prayed."
   —Mark 1:35

2. Have an honest heart.

   "Call upon me and come and pray to me, and I will listen to you. You will seek me and find me when you seek me with all your heart."—Jeremiah 29:12-13

3. Open your Bible.

   "The word of God is living and active. Sharper than any double-edged sword, it penetrates even to dividing soul and spirit, joints and marrow; it judges the thoughts and attitudes of the heart."
   —Hebrews 4:12

4. Have a genuine friend.

   "Let us consider how we may spur one another on toward love and good deeds. Let us not give up meeting together, as some are in the habit of doing, but let us encourage one another—and all the more as you see the Day approaching."—Hebrews 10:24-25

God has not meant for our lives to be empty. His plan is for us to live full and abundant lives (see John 10:10). As Rick Warren explains in his book *The Purpose-Driven Life,* "The purpose of your life is far greater than your own personal fulfillment, your peace of mind, or even your happiness. It's far greater than your family, your career, or even your wildest dreams and ambitions. If you want to know why you were placed on this planet, you must begin with God. You were born by his purpose and for his purpose."[8]

God did not make you to be empty. Walk with and in the purpose He has planned for you.

Prayer: Father God, lift me out of a life of emptiness. You didn't make me to be there, and that's not where I will remain. With Your Spirit and power I will rise above this phase of emptiness and live an abundant life. Thank You for giving me a gentle whisper. Amen.

Action: If you find yourself in an empty stage of life, put into action this week the four steps that are given.

Today's Wisdom:

Blessed is the man who trusts in the LORD,
    whose confidence is in him.
He will be like a tree planted by the water
    that sends out its roots by the stream.
It does not fear when heat comes;
    its leaves are always green.
It has no worries in a year of drought
    and never fails to bear fruit.

—JEREMIAH 17:7-8

It All Starts at Home

The quality of the time that their parents devote to them indicates to children the degree to which they are valued by their parents.... When children know that they are valued, and when they truly feel valued in the deepest parts of themselves, then they feel valuable.

—M. SCOTT PECK

It was a source of much aggravation to some fish to see a number of lobsters swimming backward instead of forward. So they called a meeting, and it was decided to start a class for the lobsters' instruction. This was done, and a number of young lobsters came. (The fish had reasoned that if they started with the young lobsters, as they grew up, they would learn to swim properly.)

At first they did very well, but afterward, when they returned home and saw their fathers and mothers swimming in the old way, they soon forgot their lessons.

So it is with many children who are well-taught at school but drift backward because of a bad home influence. Psalm 127:1–128:4 gives us some principles for building a family in which children are confident that their parents love them. First, the psalmist addresses the foundation and protection of the home: "Unless the LORD builds the house, its builders labor in vain. Unless the LORD watches over the city, the watchmen stand guard in vain" (127:1). The protective wall surrounding a city was the very first thing to be constructed when a new city was built. The people of the Old Testament knew they needed protection from their enemies, but they were also smart enough to know that walls could be climbed over, knocked down, or broken apart. They realized that their ultimate security was the Lord standing guard over the city.

Are you looking for God to help you build your home? Are you trusting the Lord to be the guard over your family? Many forces in today's society threaten the family. In Southern California we see parents who are burning the candle at both ends to provide all the material things they think will make their families happy.

We rise early and retire late, but Psalm 127:2 tells us that these efforts are futile. We are to do our best to provide for and protect our families, but we must trust first and foremost in God to take care of them.

When we tend our gardens, we're rewarded by corn, tomatoes, cucumbers, and beans. Just as the harvest of vegetables is our reward, a God-fearing child is a parent's reward. After parents tend to their children's instruction in the ways of God's wisdom and His Word, they do see the work God is doing in the lives of their offspring.

Next, comparing children to arrows in the hands of a warrior, Psalm 127:4-5 talks about how parents are to handle their offspring. Wise and skillful parents are to know their children, understand them, and carefully point them in the right direction before shooting them into the world. And, as you may have learned in an archery class, shooting an arrow straight and hitting a target is a lot harder in real life than it looks like in the movies or on TV. Likewise, godly and skillful parenting isn't easy.

The last section of today's selection teaches the importance of the Lord's presence in the home.

• The Lord blesses a home that follows His ways (Psalm 128:1-2).

- A wife who knows the Lord will be a source of beauty and life in the home (Psalm 128:3a).
- With the Lord's blessing, children will flourish like olive trees, which generously provide food, oil, and shelter (Psalm 128:3b).

Ask yourself, *What can I do to make the Lord's presence more recognizable in our home?* Or a more pointed question, *What kind of steward am I being in my home?* God has entrusted to you some very special people—your children. You will be held accountable for how you take care of them. But you're not in it alone. God offers to walk with you today and always. He provides you with guidelines like those we looked at today, plus His wisdom and His love, to help you do the job and do it well.[9]

Prayer: Father God, forgive me for the ways I shortchange my children. Help me know how to slow down the pace of life. Help me stay very aware that my children will be with me for just a short time, and that how I treat them will affect them and their children's lives too. Continue to teach me how to be the parent You want me to be. Amen.

Action: Give your child/children the gift of time—today and every day.

Today's Wisdom:

The Christian home is the Master's workshop where the processes of character-molding are silently, lovingly, faithfully, and successfully carried on.

—RICHARD M. MILNES

Thank You, Lord

*I have learned to be content
whatever the circumstances.*
—Philippians 4:11

Why wait for Thanksgiving Day to be thankful? One day a year is not enough. Every day upon waking and every evening before we nod off to sleep, these two words need to come from our mouths: "Thank You." A few years ago Bob and I wrote and gathered a collection of prayers, old and new, called *Grateful Hearts Give Thanks*. These prayers for mealtime, bedtime, and special occasions focus on how great God is and how we can bless Him by saying, "Thank You."

When we as individuals and as a united body can say thank You, we give witness to the world that we are aware that all we have comes from above. "This is the day the LORD has made; let us rejoice and be glad in it…. Give thanks to the LORD, for he is good; his love endures forever (Psalm 118:24,29).

When we have thankful hearts, our lifestyles are changed. We no longer are self-centered, trying to acquire more and more. When we do not embrace thanksgiving, we are never satisfied with what we have but need more and more. Malcontents are rarely thankful for all they have.

We read in Psalm 100:4, "Enter his gates with thanksgiving and his courts with praise; give thanks to him and praise his name." With thanks is how we enter into His presence. We must humble our hearts before approaching our good God. You can easily tell what motivates another person by how she is able to give thanks for all that she has. Ungodly people will not honor God or give thanks; they become futile in their speculations, and their foolish hearts will be darkened. (See Romans 1:21.)

"Give thanks in all circumstances, for this is God's will for you in Christ Jesus" (1 Thessalonians 5:18). Thankful believers will be content with all that God has provided. They will know that thankfulness is wanting just what they have and not wanting anymore. Spiritual thankfulness lets us say, "I don't need that," when we're tempted to purchase something that we would like but don't have the money for. It will prevent us from having that rich chocolate dessert when we are trying to lose a few pounds and inches around our waistlines.

Prayer: Father God, I can't thank You enough for all that You have given me. I have so much to be thankful for. My barns are overflowing, and grain is spilling out over the top. Thank You. Thank You. Amen.

Action: Take a risk and say "Thank You" in God's presence.

Today's Wisdom:

> For three things I thank God every day of my life: thanks that he has vouchsafed me knowledge of his works; deep thanks that he has set in my darkness the lamp of faith; deep, deepest thanks that I have another life to look forward to—a life joyous with light and flowers and heavenly song.
>
> —HELEN KELLER

Of My People Pray

If my people, who are called by my name, will humble themselves
and pray and seek my face and turn from their wicked ways,
then will I hear from heaven and will forgive their sin
and will heal their land.

—2 Chronicles 7:14

Among the many myths associated with Alexander the Great is the tale of a poor Macedonian soldier who was leading before Alexander the Great a mule laden with gold for the king's use. The mule became so tired that he could no longer carry the load, so the mule driver took it off and carried it himself, with great difficulty, for a considerable distance. Finally Alexander saw him sinking under the burden and about to throw it to the ground, so he cried out, "Friend, do not be weary yet; try to carry it to your tent, for it is now all yours."

This blessing is much better than the lottery. Who says good guys finish last? Humility certainly has its blessings. Ezra, the writer of 1 and 2 Chronicles, certainly knew the importance of humility, because he directed this passage to his people, people whom God called by name. He states that in order for God's people to receive His blessings, there are four basic requirements:

- humility
- prayer
- devotion
- repentance

This is an appropriate prayer for all of us. We shake our heads in disbelief at the depravity of mankind. Each day the headlines in the media scream out stabbings, shootings, murder, rape, and betrayal. Where have we gone wrong as a nation? Are our families breaking apart along with the moral fiber of this country? How can we get back on track to recapture the blessings of God?

Ezra says we are to humble ourselves, pray, seek God's face, and repent of our sins. Then God will

- answer our prayers,
- forgive our sins, and
- heal our land.

As you guide your family spiritually, may you recognize the truths of this passage and come to God with all humility, committing your lives again to the righteousness of God. Make a vow that in your home you will make a difference. No longer will you go along with the tide of the country. You and your family will say, "Stop! No more!"

Let's return to the timeless principles that are written in the Bible. We need families who will not only believe the Bible but also begin to live it in their daily lives. When we ask God to walk beside us, we must be willing to walk in His ways...and lead our families beside Him.

> *Prayer:* Father God, let this humility begin with my family. Give me the courage to make a difference. May each member of my family be excited about this new beginning. Amen.

Action: Read today's verse to your family at dinner tonight and see what discussion comes from it.

Today's Wisdom:

Pride changed angels into devils; humility makes men into angels.

—Augustine of Hippo

Chew like a Cow

*I meditate on your precepts
and consider your ways.*
—Psalm 119:15

We want God's time. But are we willing to give Him a portion of our day, our thoughts? Meditation takes effort, discipline, and the willingness to make space for God. We are in so much of a hurry that we just can't seem to fit meditation into our busy schedules. Oh, most of us want an intimate relationship with the Lord, but are we ready to give of our time? After all…we are busy. We've got to make more money, buy bigger toys, and race our children from one activity to another. I get tired just thinking about all the activities, don't you? Those activities and the scrambling we do to get from one to the next start to breed impatience. I've even heard people complain at a fast-food restaurant that they need to speed up the service! No wonder we aren't able to meditate on God's Word. We are in too much of a hurry.

Contrast this idea of constantly hurrying with the idea given in today's verse. It says we are to meditate on God's precepts. To meditate means to dwell on a passage. Sort of like a cow chewing her cud. Why do cows spend so much time chewing their cud? Cows first fill their stomachs with grass and other food. Then they begin the long chew-and-rechew process. It seems painfully slow, but this process turns the food into rich, creamy milk. Time consuming? Yes. But it's a must if you want good milk. That's the way it is with us Christians. If we want to grow, we must slow down and meditate on God's principles. We need to read His precious truths, then ponder their meaning and influence and wonder. Take comfort in knowing that there is rest and renewal for all of us when we meditate on God's precepts.

> *Prayer:* Father God, thank You for giving me a quiet time so I can meditate on Your words. Your principles have given me such peace—for one thing, I've wanted to slow down. Amen.

> *Action:* Slow down—meditate. Chew on God's Word and truths.

Today's Wisdom:

> True spiritual maturity, the product of time spent in the Word and continuous walking in the Spirit, manifests itself when Christ's will and your will are synonymous.

> —Tim LaHaye

Finding Favor in God's Eyes

Noah found favor in the eyes of the LORD....
Noah did everything just as God commanded him.
—GENESIS 6:8,22

One way to find favor with God is to love His little children. In the New Testament we read where Jesus loved the young children and warned us as adults to be careful not to harm the little children. As a grandparent, I can gain favor with God by being kind and gentle with the little ones in our family. What an honor to be a part of the spiritual development of any child.

In government, sports, business, medicine, education, theater, and music—there are those who rise to the top of their professions and are honored because they find favor through their actions, personalities, efforts, or sometimes just because of their social connections. They might be known for very amazing and noble accomplishments like running a nonprofit, discovering a new cancer drug, teaching those thought unteachable, or singing the most beautiful aria the world has ever heard.

These are all remarkable reasons to have favor among men. But have you ever thought how much richer life would be to have God find favor with you as a parent, a grandparent? I stand in awe when I think of God finding favor with me, but He does.

Noah lived in a world much like today's, a world full of sin. Humanity hasn't changed much over the centuries—we just give sin a different name. Yet through all this wickedness, Noah was a person who lived a godly life. His life was pleasing to God even during those evil days.

Noah didn't find favor because of his individual goodness but through his obedience to God. We are also judged according to the same standard—that of our personal faith and obedience.

Even though Noah was upright and blameless before God, he wasn't perfect. God recognized that Noah's life reflected a genuine faith, but not always a perfect faith. Do you sometimes feel all alone in your walk with God? I know I do. Noah found that it wasn't the surroundings of his life that kept him in close fellowship with God, but it was the heart of Noah that qualified him to find friendship with God.

It isn't important to find favor from our fellow humans. God's favor is so much more rewarding. Somehow God's favor with me is passed down through the favor from my grandchildren. As we live in this very difficult time of history, I might ask, "Do I find favor in God's sight?" God gives us grace to live victoriously: "He gives us more grace" (James 4:6).

Prayer: Father God, let my eyes always be upon You and not the applause of my fellow humans. Mankind's honor will someday pass away, but Your honor is eternal. Thank You for honoring me through my legacy of family. Amen.

Action: Do something today that draws attention more to God than to yourself.

Today's Wisdom:

The world is a looking-glass, and gives back to every

man the reflection of his own face. Frown at it, and it in turn will look sourly at you, laugh at it, and with it, and it's a jolly, kind companion.

—WILLIAM MAKEPEACE THACKERAY

Fear of the Lord

The fear of the LORD is the beginning of wisdom;
all who follow his precepts have good understanding.
To him belongs eternal praise.
—PSALM 111:10

The motto of the wisdom teachers is that the fear of the LORD (showing holy respect and reverence for God and shunning evil) is the starting point and essence of wisdom. When you have a fear of the LORD, you express that respect by submission to His will.

- "Behold, the fear of the Lord, that is wisdom; and to depart from evil is understanding."—Job 28:28 NASB
- "The fear of the LORD is the beginning of wisdom, and the knowledge of the Holy One is understanding."—Proverbs 9:10 NASB
- "The fear of the LORD is the instruction for wisdom, and before honor comes humility."—Proverbs 15:33 NASB
- "The conclusion, when all has been heard, is: fear God and keep His commandments, because this applies to every person." —Ecclesiastes 12:13 NASB

Wisdom is not acquired by a mechanical formula, but through a right relationship with God. It seems that following God's principles and commandments should be the obvious conclusion of our thankfulness for all He has done for us.

In today's church world, many people have lost the concept of fearing God. The soft side of Christianity has preached only the "love of God." We haven't balanced the scale by teaching the other side, His justice and judgment—fear, anger, wrath, obedience, and punishment. Just because some pastors don't teach it from their pulpits doesn't make it less a reality. As with involvement with drugs, alcohol, lust, and envy, we must respect the consequences of our actions, or we will be destroyed by them. Our safeguard to resist these life destroyers is to have a proper respect for God. Then we will be obedient to His precepts and stay away from the fire of temptation. God lights the way for our paths, but we must be willing to follow His lighted path.

Prayer: Father God, fill me with an awesome respect for You. I want to be obedient to Your mighty precepts. Amen.

Action: Exhibit a new respect for your all-powerful God.

Today's Wisdom:

Get wisdom, get understanding;
do not forget my words or swerve from them.
Do not forsake wisdom, and she will protect you;...
Wisdom is supreme; therefore get wisdom.
Though it cost all you have, get understanding.

—PROVERBS 4:5,7

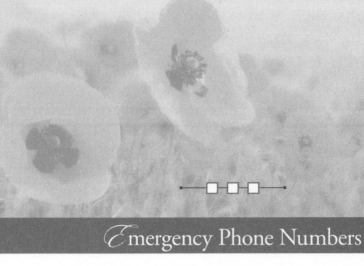

Emergency Phone Numbers

O Lord, hear me praying; listen to my plea, O God my King,
for I will never pray to anyone but you.
—PSALM 5:1 TLB

With cell phones we can make urgent calls to business or family contacts in a flash. But at times there are emergency calls that need to be made that don't require a phone. The numbers for these calls are found in the Bible.

Emergency Phone Numbers

When in sorrow, call John 14.
When men fail you, call Psalm 27.
If you want to be fruitful, call John 15.
When you have sinned, call Psalm 51.
When you worry, call Matthew 6:19-34.
When you are in danger, call Psalm 91.
When God seems far away, call Psalm 139.
When your faith needs stirring, call Hebrews 11.
When you are lonely and fearful, call Psalm 23.
When you grow bitter and critical, call 1 Corinthians 13.

For Paul's secret to happiness, call Colossians 3:12-17.

For understanding of Christianity, call 2 Corinthians 5:15-19.

When you feel down and out, call Romans 8:31.

When you want peace and rest, call Matthew 11:25-30.

When the world seems bigger than God, call Psalm 90.

When you want Christian assurance, call Romans 8:1-30.

When you leave home for labor or travel, call Psalm 121.

When your prayers grow narrow or selfish, call Psalm 67.

For a great invention/opportunity, call Isaiah 55.

When you want courage for a task, call Joshua 1.

For how to get along with fellow men, call Romans 12.

When you think of investments and returns, call Mark 10.

If you are depressed, call Psalm 27.

If your pocketbook is empty, call Psalm 37.

If people seem unkind, call John 15.

If discouraged about your work, call Psalm 126.

If you find the world growing small and yourself great, call
Psalm 19.

—AUTHOR UNKNOWN

Emergency numbers may be dialed direct. No operator assistance is necessary. All lines to heaven are open 24 hours a day and seven days a week.

Prayer: Father God, You say to call on You, that You will never forsake me. Thank You for giving me the Bible so I can be encouraged in times of emergency. Amen.

Action: Call one of the emergency phone numbers today to see what information you receive.

Today's Wisdom:

> Without wise leadership, a nation is in trouble; but with good counselors there is safety.

> —Proverbs 11:14 TLB

A Place of Togetherness

*I will give thanks to the LORD with all my heart, in the
company of the upright and in the assembly.*

—Psalm 111:1 NASB

At our church on Thanksgiving morning, we have an early service filled with music and praises. Members of our fellowship flock to the roving microphone to share their thanksgiving with others in attendance. We hear amazing stories of how God has lifted up various members throughout the year. Often the pastor has to cut off the time of togetherness to make room for those attending the next service.

Is your home a place of togetherness? What can you do today that will encourage togetherness instead of working against it? Let's make togetherness happen today. Little touches around the home can make a big difference. The way the furniture is arranged, for example, can tell a lot about your priorities. Are there comfortable groupings for conversation? Does every seat have an adequate lighting source and a place for each person to set their hot coffee/tea or cold drink?

Another consideration is the location of the TV. Many family rooms these days are set up with every chair pointed at the TV set. For other families it is the computer that seems to consume everybody's attention. I know some families that keep their TV on a wheeled cart in a closet, ready to roll out for those occasions that warrant the family's viewing, but otherwise it is stored away during ordinary family evenings. Setting computer hours and keeping those boundaries in place is a way to control that major distraction.

What matters is that we share our lives by talking, listening, reflecting, playing games, and engaging in mutual activities. Such togetherness fills our homes with a warm fireside glow with or without the fire. This is living out faith in such a practical, loving way. And when you make God the center of the home, it is easier to arrange all the other details!

Prayer: Father God, every mother's desire is to have her family together. I know that my greatest moments in life are when everyone is around the dining-room table enjoying a home-cooked meal. Thank You for a family that enjoys being together. Amen.

Action: Bring out one of your favorite games tonight and play it with the family. No TV allowed.

Today's Wisdom:

Home is the one place in all this world where hearts are sure of each other. It is the place of confidence. It is the place where we tear off that mask of guarded and suspicious coldness which the world forces us to wear in self-defense, and where we pour out the unreserved communications of full and confiding hearts. It is the spot where expressions of tenderness gush out without any sensation of awkwardness and without any dread of ridicule.

—FREDERICK W. ROBERTSON

Celebrate to Celebrate

Give thanks to the LORD, for he is good;
his love endures forever.
—Psalm 107:1

I've often been accused of celebrating just to celebrate. I guess that's correct, because I've built a ministry on telling women how to develop a close-knit family. My experience has shown that healthy families love to celebrate—you name it; they celebrate.

Make celebrations a tradition in your family! Why not? Life is for living, and in the living there's always something to celebrate. Celebrate everything—good days, bad days that are finally over, birthdays, and even half birthdays. Get your children involved preparing for a dinner celebration. Make it special. Let them make place cards, set the table, help you cook, create a centerpiece. Our children were always assigned to greet our guests at the door—a wonderful opportunity for teaching hospitality and manners.

Let your sharing extend beyond your family. Several times a year, create a "love basket" filled with food for a family in need. Try spending part of your holidays helping out at a shelter or a mission. This has been one of our most rewarding celebrations.

Present your own version of a You Are Special plate to a special guest, and have her use it for her meal. Let the recipient know that she is special and is loved by all. Go around the table and tell that special person why she is so special. Have a box of Kleenex ready—the tears will flow. In some cases it will be the first time she has been told that she is special and loved at the same time.

Don't be limited. Look for ways to celebrate life and those you love!

Prayer: Father God, there are a lot of reasons to celebrate today. Let me be a helper for those who want to celebrate but don't know how. Amen.

Action: Plan a celebration for someone you love.

Today's Wisdom:

> Be it health or be it leisure,
> Be it skill we have to give,
> Still in spending it for others
> Christians only really live.
> Not in having or receiving,
> But in giving, there is bliss;
> He who has no other pleasure
> Ever may rejoice in this.

—AUTHOR UNKNOWN

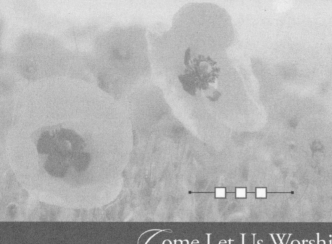

Come Let Us Worship

Come, let us bow down in worship,
let us kneel before the LORD our Maker.
—Psalm 95:6

A recent point of frustration, debate, and tension in many churches has been about defining worship and agreeing what it should look like. Older Christians are confused because of changes made to the style of worship. They wonder whatever happened to the old hymns that were so beloved. They knew the page numbers and all the old verses by heart. Today there are no hymnals, the organs have been silenced, and guitars, drums, and cymbals have taken over. The choir and their robes have been abandoned, and now we have five to seven singers on stage leading songs. We stand for 30 minutes at a time singing song lyrics that we aren't familiar with from a large screen. What's happening? If the church doesn't have these components, the young people leave and go to where it's happening. Are we going to let the form of worship divide our churches? I hope not!

The origins of many of the different expressions of worship can be found in the Psalms, which portray worship as an act of the whole person, not just the mental sphere. The early founders established ways to worship based on what they perceived after reading this great book of the Bible. Over the centuries, Christian worship has taken many different forms, involving various expressions and postures on the part of churchgoers.

The Hebrew word for "worship" literally means "to kneel" or "to bow down." The act of worship is the gesture of humbling oneself before a mighty authority. The Psalms also call upon us to "sing to the LORD, bless His name" (96:2 NASB). Music has always played a large part in the sacred act of worship.

Physical gestures and movements are also mentioned in the Psalms. Lifting our hands before God signifies our adoration of Him. Clapping our hands shows our celebration before God. Some worshipers rejoice in His presence with tambourines and dancing (see Psalm 150:4). To worship like the psalmist is to obey Jesus' command to "love the Lord your God with all your heart and with all your soul and with all your mind and with all your strength" (Mark 12:30). There are many more insights for worship in the book of Psalms:

- God's gifts of instruments and vocal music can be used to help us worship (47:1; 81:1-4).
- We can appeal to God for help, and we can thank Him for His deliverance (4:3; 17:1-5).
- Difficult times should not prevent us from praising God (22:23-24; 102:1-2; 140:4-8).
- We are to celebrate what God has done for us (18; 106; 136).[10]

Prayer: Father God, give me insight into what form of worship is pleasing to You. I don't want to be negative in my church regarding how we come to You and worship. Amen.

Action: Pray about this new division in our churches. Be
willing to create harmony, not discord.

Today's Wisdom:

> It is in the whole process of meeting and solving
> problems that life has meaning. Problems are the
> cutting edge that distinguishes between success
> and failure. Problems call forth our courage and
> our wisdom; indeed, they create our courage and
> our wisdom. It is only because of problems that
> we grow mentally and spiritually. It is through the
> pain of confronting and resolving problems that
> we learn.
>
> —M. SCOTT PECK

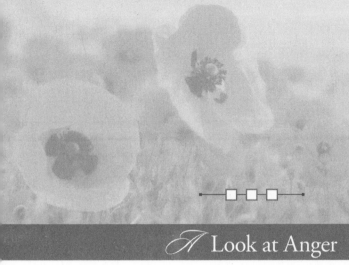

A Look at Anger

Sensible people control their temper;
they earn respect by overlooking wrongs.
—PROVERBS 19:11 NLT

Anger burns like a wild brushfire. As I read my daily newspaper and view the TV news, I am constantly reminded of the sin of anger. It emerges in so many different ways, but the cause is always clear—lack of control.

A healthy relationship cannot coexist with anger. The two do not go together. In order for our friendships to flourish, we must be able to control this raging fire that exists in most human beings. The book of Proverbs gives some insight concerning anger. The following passages are all from *The Living Bible*.

- "A short-tempered man is a fool. He hates the man who is patient" (14:17).

- "A quick-tempered man starts fights; a cool-tempered man tries to stop them" (15:18).

- "It is better to be slow-tempered than famous; it is better to have self-control than to control an army" (16:32).

- "A fool gets into constant fights. His mouth is his undoing! His words endanger him" (18:6-7).

- "A short-tempered man must bear his own penalty; you can't do much to help him. If you try once you must try a dozen times!" (19:19).

- "Keep away from angry, short-tempered men, lest you learn to be like them and endanger your soul" (22:24-25).

- "A rebel shouts in anger; a wise man holds his temper in and cools it" (29:11).

- "There is more hope for a fool than for a man of quick temper" (29:20).

- "A hot-tempered man starts fights and gets into all kinds of trouble" (29:22).

If anger is one of your enemies, go to God in prayer and ask for healing. It is a disease like cancer and can destroy your body if not addressed. Do not wait until it is too late. Healthy relationships demand that anger be conquered.[11]

Prayer: Father God, let me examine myself to see if there is any evidence of anger. If so, I want to give it to You. May You help me conquer this dragon that wants to destroy me. Amen.

Action: Examine yourself to see if there is any anger in your soul.

Today's Wisdom:

Be ye angry, and sin not; therefore all anger is not sinful; I suppose because some degree of it, and upon some occasions, is inevitable. It become sinful, or contradicts, however, the rule of Scripture, when it is conceived upon slight and inadequate provocation, and when it continues long.

—WILLIAM PALEY

*H*ear the Bells

Ascribe to the LORD the glory due his name;
worship the LORD in the splendor of his holiness.
—Psalm 29:2

A young man from a West Texas farm community received a football scholarship from a small college in Texas. He was so excited about this new adventure. After he packed his bags to take to school, his mother came to say goodbye. After hugs and tears she asked her son to make her one promise. "Be sure to attend church every Sunday while you are away from home." With no hesitation he assured Mama that he would honor that request.

After settling in to his dorm, he met several incoming freshman whom he liked; however, these young men had little if any spiritual interests. One of the boys came from a wealthy farm family nearby and invited his new friend to come home with him for the weekend to hunt and fish. Of course, this small-town farmboy said, "Yes, that will be fun."

On Sunday morning as they were mounting up on their horses to take them where the hunting and fishing were good, the young man heard the loud bell-ringing from a nearby church. They rode on farther toward their day's adventure when again the young man heard a fainter ringing of the church bells. Going farther toward their destination and farther from the church bells, this young man again heard the church bells ring, but this time the sound was very faint. He stopped his horse and told his host he had to go back and attend church. The host said, "We don't have to go to church today. Let's go on, and I will go to church with you next week." The young Texan replied, "No, I must go back while I can still hear the bells."

Are you in that young man's situation where you once heard God's strong voice but today you have moved away from God and His voice has become fainter and fainter? Your conscience might be calling out, "Go back while you can still hear the voice of God!"

As it is said, "If you feel far away from God, guess who moved?" Return to Him before you no longer hear His voice calling you to come back home.

Prayer: Father God, continue to ring the bell loud and clear. I never want to stop hearing Your call. Prevent everything that would hinder me from hearing Your voice. Amen.

Action: How clear do you hear the bell ring? If it's not clear, you will want to turn back again to your first love.

Today's Wisdom:

Worship depends not upon our own activities, but upon the activities which God brings to bear upon us; to them we are forced to react as worshipers.

—KENNETH E. KIRK

A Mirror of Jesus

To this you were called, because Christ suffered for you,
leaving you an example,
that you should follow in his steps.
—1 PETER 2:21

Many years ago I read a book called *In His Steps.* It was the story of a man who for a period of time attempted to walk in the steps of Jesus. Everything he said, everywhere he went, all decisions he made were done as if he were Jesus. As you can imagine, it was just about impossible. However, the experience changed this man's life forever.

We are not Jesus—nor will we ever be. Yet Jesus left us with His example of a godly life. As we walk through life on earth, we will experience daily situations that will reveal our character. Jesus gives us the example of kindness and gentleness. He was full of sympathy and affection and always loved with mercy.

Jesus understands our pain and grief and the tragedy of friends who betray us. He knows that we live in a world where others suffer sickness and commit sin that we can do nothing about. He cares and wants to help us. He wants to cleanse us and heal us. As the Lord lives in us, He will form us into the beautiful, marvelous image of God according to our own uniqueness.

As a parent or grandparent, the only Jesus your children or grand-children might see is you. You will reflect the character of God to these young impressionable treasures. They will catch more often what you are rather than what you say. Their little eyes are like a lighthouse beam always searching the dark night.

No, we can't be Jesus. But we can develop a teachable spirit. We can love Him and desire Him in our hearts with all our souls, minds, and spirits. We will then find ourselves transformed into giving, loving spirits with the joy of Jesus in our hearts. Our characters will then reveal the likeness of Jesus. Our spirits will help the helpless, pray for the sick, feed and clothe the homeless, and support those whom God lifts up to be missionaries where we can't go.

As we walk in His steps, as we follow His call for us today, let us see every possible way to express His love.

Prayer: Father God, may I be challenged to walk in Your steps. Reveal to me what I should do to be a loving and caring person. I want Your vision to be mine also. Help me to be a reflection of You to the children and people in my life. Amen.

Action: Ask yourself, "Are the qualities of Jesus evident in my life?"

Today's Wisdom:

Words are more powerful than perhaps anyone suspects, and once deeply engraved in a child's mind, they are not easily eradicated.

—May Sarton

Life is an opportunity, benefit from it.
Life is beauty, admire it.
Life is bliss, taste it.
Life is a dream, realize it.
Life is a challenge, meet it.
Life is a duty, complete it.
Life is a game, play it.
Life is a promise, fulfill it.
Life is sorrow, overcome it.
Life is a song, sing it.
Life is a struggle, accept it.
Life is a tragedy, confront it.
Life is an adventure, dare it.
Life is luck, make it.
Life is too precious, do not destroy it.
Life is life, fight for it.

—MOTHER TERESA

What Do You Say?

Praise the LORD, O my soul;
all my inmost being, praise his holy name.
Praise the LORD, O my soul,
and forget not all his benefits.
—PSALM 103:1-2

Two great words in the English language are "thank you." At an early age we begin to tell our children to say thank you. When someone gives them a gift or a compliment and before they can utter these two words, we jump right in and remind them, "What do you say?" However, as we grow from childhood to adulthood, we often forget our manners and hold back from expressing our appreciation to someone who does us a service.

It's the same way with God. He loves to hear and know that we are thankful for all He bestows upon us. God is the provider of all we have. In Ecclesiastes 2:24-25 we read, "There is nothing better for a man than to eat and drink and tell himself that his labor is good. This also I have seen that it is from the hand of God. For who can eat and who can have enjoyment without Him?" (NASB).

Thankful hearts give thanks. One way to express our thanks for our food is to give a blessing each time we have a meal. Our family always gives a blessing of grace before we eat. This is a tradition at home or out at a restaurant. We never want to forget where our food comes from. We never want to take for granted the things we receive daily that make life and living possible.

As I have gotten older, I look back over this short life and realize that God has been faithful all along the way. He has always provided for all our "needs." Our "wants" are not always provided, but our needs are. "His divine power has given us everything we need for life and godliness through our knowledge of him who called us by his own glory and goodness" (2 Peter 1:3).

We humbly reach out to God with thanksgiving and praise. One of the leading indicators of our spiritual walk with God is our thankfulness for all that He has done for us. Paul shares with us in Romans 1:21: "For although they knew God, they neither glorified him as God nor gave thanks to him, but their thinking became futile and their foolish hearts were darkened."

This verse should be a red flag for us women. It is a warning that if we forget who God is, our foolish hearts will be darkened. Oh no, not all at once, but small decisions over a period of time will lead us away from our God. We must guard our hearts so they don't turn inward, but so our heartbeats lead us away from ourselves and toward others.

In Paul's writings he tells us to be content in all situations (see Philippians 4:11). When we are restless and find ourselves discontent with our lives and our situations, it is accentuated when we don't have a heart that gives thanks. "Be joyful always; pray continually; give thanks in all circumstances, for this is God's will for you in Christ Jesus" (1 Thessalonians 5:16-18).

Let's not take anything for granted. The big things are easy to recall, because they are the biggies; the small things—air, water, home, spouse, food, children—these are often overlooked because we just assume they are there. In everything give thanks.

Prayer: Father God, don't let me forget to always be thankful for what You do for me. You are a gracious God who continually pours out blessings on my life. Thank You for everything—big and small. Amen.

Action: Evaluate your thankful heart. How could it be improved?

Today's Wisdom:

To be thankful for what I have received, and for what my Lord has prepared, is the surest way to receive more.

—ANDREW MURRAY

Surround Your Home with Prayer

If you make the Most High your dwelling—
even the LORD, who is my refuge—
then no harm will befall you,
no disaster will come near your tent.
—PSALM 91:9-10

Many times when a family moves into a new home, there is a prayer of dedication not only for the home, but for each room individually. If someone you know is ready for this transition or even if you want to bless your longtime home for the first time, it is a great way to invite God into a home and into the lives of those who inhabit its rooms. Collect a small group of family and friends, go into each room, and pray for the activities that will go on in that particular room. You might have different individuals pray for a protective hedge as you enter each room. Those families who have done this express what a sense of peace falls over them when they realize that their closest of friends are concerned enough about their new residence that they are willing to support them in dedicating their new home to the Lord.

With so many couples working outside the home, it is important that we pray hedges around our homes as well as hedges for each individual in our homes, so that no evil or harm shall befall them. As our society continues to devalue our family structure, we need to place an even greater emphasis on prayers of protection. Husbands, wives, and children are bombarded by influences that destroy the love they have for one another, their focus on the Lord, their prayer lives, their commitment to church, their consistency in Bible reading, and their relationships with family and friends.

Make it a habit to continually be in prayer for your mate and children as you go through the day. Share with one another your schedules, so you know when extra prayer support is needed. When traveling away from home, be sure to take some reminders from home—a family picture, a present that was given before departing, artwork from the children, a Bible—anything to help you focus on what's really important to you.

My Bob has told me on several occasions how my prayers have given him strength and encouragement when he was away from the family. These family reminders make it a lot easier to say no when one might fall into temptation due to being lonely and away from the family.

Prayer: Father God, I pray that You will protect our family from all evil. Build a protective hedge around our lives. Amen.

Action: Make it a habit to pray for your family each day.

Today's Wisdom:

One truth about God which I continue to discover anew is that he has more for us than we can imagine. His plans far exceed our plans, and his grace makes possible so much more than we can envision.

—Nancy Pickering

The Symbol of the Cross

Those who passed by hurled insults at him,
shaking their heads and saying,
"You who are going to destroy the temple and
build it in three days, save yourself!
Come down from the cross, if you are the Son of God!"
—MATTHEW 27:39-40

In those days the cross needed no explanation, for the Jews had seen thousands of their countrymen crucified by the Romans. Many of the early followers of Jesus were crucified. Over the centuries the cross has become the symbol of Christian belief. As the Star of David signifies the Jewish believer, so the cross represents a Christian believer.

Designers of fine jewelry have fashioned beautiful necklaces in the shape of a cross; at the top of mountaintops we see a cross erected as a symbol of Christianity; we journey to a military cemetery and see the graves marked with white crosses; most Christian churches have a steeple with a cross perched on top of the building.

What has the event of the Cross given to us as believers? Read Romans 8:1-16:

- No condemnation—v. 1

- Freedom—v. 2
- Destruction of sin—v. 3
- The Holy Spirit—v. 5
- Life and peace—v. 6
- Eternal life—v. 10-11
- Acceptance as God's child—v. 14
- Confidence in the Spirit—v. 16

Without the cross and the resurrection there would be no reason to have faith. Our hope and assurance of salvation would be like a puff of air. It would offer no more than any other religious teaching. Without the cross it would be foolish for us to believe.

We must make a decision every day to follow after the cross of Jesus. In Matthew 16:24 we read, "Then Jesus said to his disciples, 'If anyone would come after me, he must deny himself and take up his cross and follow me.'" Jesus knew that following Him would come with a price. As individuals, we would have to *choose* to follow Him. He would not force you or me to be His servant.

"For the word of the cross is foolishness to those who are perishing, but to us who are being saved it is the power of God" (1 Corinthians 1:18 NASB). In this verse Paul shows that worldly wisdom, which the Corinthians prized so highly, is the very antithesis (opposite) of the wisdom of God. The world says that the cross is foolish, but the Christian believer recognizes this message as the very power of God.

The cross symbol is far more than a symbol. Throughout Christian history it has been the one sign of unity that bonds all believers. The cross has come under attack by all who want to destroy the message of Jesus. Even today some of our government agencies have attempted to remove all crosses from our government buildings. The world doesn't want any reminders of our Christian heritage. But what God has preserved for more than two thousand years He is able to maintain until He returns for His Church.

Prayer: Father God, may I see more than a symbol when I see the cross. May I appreciate what Your Son has done for me, a sinner. Without the cross and the resurrection there would be no Christian faith. Thank You for the cross. Amen.

Action: When you see a cross, remember what it represents and the price that Jesus paid for us.

Today's Wisdom:

Life doesn't begin at twenty, or at forty, but at the Cross of Calvary.

—ELAINE KILGORE

Don't Forget the Past

From childhood you have known the sacred writings
which are able to give you the wisdom that leads to
salvation through faith which is in Christ Jesus.
—2 Timothy 3:15 NASB

If I had my school days to relive, I would concentrate more on history—not only U.S. history, but the history of the world. Throughout Scripture we are told to remember our pasts. We are the current result of all our pasts, not only from world history but from all our ancestors.

I'm overwhelmed when I realize that my ancestors weren't all killed by war or disease. My family is here today because of a miracle of survival. We have a purpose. Have you taken time to consider what your purpose might be?

We are challenged not to forget what matters. Paul writes in 2 Timothy 1:5-8, "I remind you to kindle afresh the gift of God which is in you through the laying on of my hands. For God has not given us a spirit of timidity, but of power and love and discipline" (NASB).

In these latter days we as believers will be called on to stand up and give witness to Jesus and what He has done through history. We are told that during the last days men will:

• ignore God

- love things and possessions
- use people
- play religious games
- be boastful and proud
- have children who are disobedient to parents
- become ungrateful
- will consider nothing sacred

This is certainly a list for today. Every day I am reminded that we Christians have forgotten our history. How then are we to recover the past?

- Follow Paul's example.

  "But you, Timothy, certainly know what I teach, and how I live, and what my purpose in life is. You know my faith, my patience, my love, and my endurance."

  —2 Timothy 3:10 NLT

- Remain in God's Word.

  "You must remain faithful to the things you have been taught. You know they are true, for you know you can trust those who taught you. You have been taught the holy Scriptures from childhood, and they have given you the wisdom to receive the salvation that comes by trusting in Christ Jesus. All Scripture is inspired by God and is useful to teach us what is true and to make us realize what is wrong in our lives. It corrects us when we are wrong and teaches us to do what is right. God uses it to prepare and equip his people to do every good work."

  —2 Timothy 3:14-17 NLT

- Complete your calling.

  "Preach the word of God. Be prepared whether the time is favorable or not."

  —2 Timothy 4:2 NLT

- Remember who is at the finish line.

    "Remember, we will all stand before the judgment seat of God. For the Scriptures say, 'As surely as I live,' says the LORD, 'every knee will bow to me and every tongue will confess allegiance to God.' Yes, each of us will give a personal account to God."

    —Romans 14:10-12 NLT

We must not forget our past. Biblical history lets us rest assured that God has a master plan for all of history. We are not able to know what that master plan is, for God's thoughts are bigger than our thoughts. We are not able to understand every event in history, but because we know who God is, we can be at peace with all situations. Let us know our past so we can face the future with confidence.

Prayer: Father God, give me a desire to know my history. Help me to understand the present and trust the future. Give me a desire to search out and find my purpose in life.

Action: Consider reading Rick Warren's book *The Purpose-Driven Life*. Take time sharing about your family history with your children. Inspire their interest in their family legacies.

Today's Wisdom:

Long before you were conceived by your parents, you were conceived in the mind of God.

—RICK WARREN

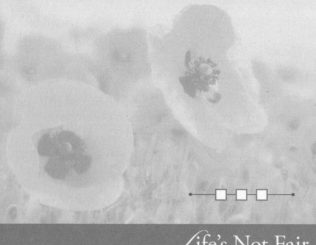

*L*ife's Not Fair

It is God who judges:
He brings one down, he exalts another.
—Psalm 75:7

*Y*ou've heard the expression "It's who you know that counts." Depending upon your experiences in life, you might say, "Right on; so true." Others may shout, "That's not fair!" because this principle seems contrary to fair play and competition. "It's who you know" doesn't give people of equal abilities an equal opportunity for success. But I've come to realize that—as much as I would like to believe otherwise—the truth is that life isn't fair. It never has been, and it never will be until we get to heaven.

Being known by the right person does shorten some of the processes of life. Having a good relationship with your banker speeds up the loan process. Always using the same pharmacist may mean you won't have to stand in line. Knowing your pastor may make planning your wedding easier. Being acquainted with your mechanic may save you money on car repairs. Knowing the right person can make life easier.

It's very important to forge good relationships with people who work to provide the services you depend on. Knowing the right person does open doors for you. Take time to develop these relationships. They pay great dividends in life. When we had to relocate to a new city, after 31 years in our previous city, we had to create new relationships with the service sector. A new banker, a new pastor, a new plumber, a new electrician—we are slowly building a network of new relationships. We sought out fair and honest providers, and in turn we tried to be loyal and friendly clients.

In Psalm 75:7, we read that the Lord "brings down one, and exalts another." The almighty God is behind the scenes giving His own kind of breaks, opportunities, and promotions—all according to His mercy and grace. Because we know Him, we are privileged to experience many opportunities that the secular world does not have.

The resources of God are at our disposal, as is His unlimited power to work for our good through all circumstances. Being in relationship with God through our Lord Jesus Christ does matter. Knowing *the* right person—Jesus—permits us to receive a lot of promises that are available only to His children. Thank God we know who we know.

Prayer: Father God, knowing You has been the best connection of my life. You have been with me when I've been alone. Your promises are all I will ever need. Amen.

Action: Take advantage of knowing God. Accept His many blessings.

Today's Wisdom:

After Benjamin Franklin received a letter thanking him for a kindness, he replied: "As to the kindness you mention, I wish I could have been of more service to you than I have been, but if I had, the only thanks that I should desire are that you would always be ready to serve any other person that may need your assistance, and so let good offices go around, for mankind are all of a family. As for my own part, when I am employed in serving others I do not look upon myself as conferring favors but paying debts."

A Purpose for Life

Even when I am old and gray,
do not forsake me, O God,
till I declare your power to the next generation,
your might to all who are to come.

—Psalm 71:18

There are seasons of life that cause us to think more about the hereafter. When we hit milestone birthdays or someone in our life enters the elder years, we start to wonder, *What happens when we die?* The psalmist pleads for God not to forsake him until he declares the power of God to the next generation. Wow! What a great prayer. I guess that's why I do what I do. I want to tell everyone, starting with my immediate family and branching out to others, about the power and might of God.

One of my theme verses while walking through Cancerland the last seven years has been John 11:4, which reads, "This sickness will not end in death. No, it is for God's glory so that God's Son may be glorified through it." With every speaking opportunity, I share what the power of God has done in my healing process. I want to give testimony to the greatness of my almighty God. I have so much to tell. I pray for God to give me a message, a passion for the message, power to tell the message, and an audience who wants to hear of God's power and might.

Lee Iacocca, former CEO of Chrysler Corporation, reflects on life after death in his book *Talking Straight*. He expresses these thoughts:

> As I get older, I think more and more about what comes next. I know there's got to be something else after this life is over, because I can't grasp the alternative. I can't imagine that through all eternity I'll never see anyone I love again, that my whole awareness will be obliterated. I can't believe that we're only bodies passing through....
>
> I haven't yet formed a clear idea about what the hereafter might be like. I don't know if everyone's an angel. Or an apparition. Or it's just all beyond comprehension. But I do hope that it's going to be better than here, because life on this planet is not exactly peaches and cream. I mean, this life is tough. I suppose that's the promise religion holds out. If you can take this life as it comes and give it your best, there will be something better afterwards.[12]

Don't wait until you are old and gray. Begin today to share the message of Jesus Christ with the whole world. Whether you want reassurance or are new to belief in salvation, take time to read some of God's holy words regarding this phase of one's life. Read:

- Luke 18:13
- Luke 23:43
- John 10:28
- John 14:2-3
- Acts 16:30-31
- Romans 6:23
- Romans 10:9-10
- Ephesians 2:8-9

You can receive Christ right now by faith through this prayer:

Father God, I need You. Thank You for sending Your Son, Jesus, to die on the cross for my sins. I open the door of my life and receive Him as my personal Savior and Lord. Thank You for forgiving my sins and giving me eternal life. Take control of the throne of my life. Make me the kind of person You want me to be. I ask this in Your Son's name, Jesus. Amen.

If you prayed this prayer, read the following Scriptures for your assurance:

- John 14:21
- 1 John 5:11-13
- Hebrews 13:5
- Revelation 3:20

Action: Write in the front page of your Bible today's date. Never doubt the decision you made.

Today's Wisdom:

Take my heart
and make it
Your dwelling place
so that everyone
I touch
will be touched also
by You!

—ALICE JOYCE DAVIDSON

When Bad Times Roll

God is our refuge and strength,
always ready to help in times of trouble.
So we will not fear when earthquakes come
and the mountains crumble into the sea.

—Psalm 46:1-2 NLT

On December 26, 2004, the world was shocked when a 9.0 earthquake off the western coast of Sumatra in Southeast Asia caused a tsunami to crash ashore, killing hundreds of thousands of people and destroying entire towns. As the devastating news reached the world, people cried out, "Where were You, God?" We always ask this "why" question because our inquiring minds want to know why a loving God permits such death, particularly when the toll included many children. We must remember that we live in a fallen world where death is a part of our human experience. Terrible events can happen because of the laws of nature that are set in motion. They can happen because of the sins of mankind. They can happen because trouble and suffering are beyond our control. But God does not abandon us in such times. And when we face devastation or see it played out in such overwhelmingly sad ways, God's Word gives us comfort.

In today's verse we find three comforts in such events of life:

- God is our refuge.
- God is our strength.
- God is always ready to help in times of trouble.

If we can internalize these three big promises, we will own this victory: We will not live in fear. What great assurances when our souls quake! We can apply these to all events of life, whether tsunamis, earthquakes, heartbreaks, or soul quakes.

When we walk though life's storms, we have two alternatives: we can respond as a faithless person or as a faith-filled person. A faith-filled person

- delights in reading and knowing God's Word;
- meditates on God's law day and night;
- will be like a tree firmly planted by streams of water that yields fruit in its season; and
- will prosper in all things.

> Blessed is the man
>   who does not walk in the counsel of the wicked
> or stand in the way of sinners
>   or sit in the seat of mockers.
> But his delight is in the law of the LORD,
>   and on his law he meditates day and night.
> He is like a tree planted by streams of water,
>   which yields its fruit in season
> and whose leaf does not wither.
>   Whatever he does prospers.
>
> —PSALM 1:1-3

This person of faith understands where she came from and where she is going. She is not one who questions God because of the events of the world. She doesn't look to the world for the answers of life. She is firmly grounded in what God has to say about assurance when the quakes of life occur. This Psalm 1 passage contrasts a faith-filled person with the faithless person. In verses 4-6 we read:

> The wicked are not so,
> but they are like chaff which the wind drives away,
> therefore the wicked will not stand in the judgment,
> nor sinners in the assembly of the righteous,
> but the way of the wicked will perish (NASB).

Who among us would choose the end of the faithless person? Yes, we have two choices in how we deal with the quakes of life. Either the choice of faith or the choice of faithlessness. "But as for me and my household, we will serve the LORD" (Joshua 24:15).

Prayer:　Father God, let me stand on Your promises when the quakes of life come my way (as they surely will). Give me the faith to trust Your Word. Let me lead my family into this trust. Amen.

Action:　Begin today to trust God and all His promises for you and your family. Reread Psalm 1:2-3.

Today's Wisdom:

Be still, and know that I am God.

—PSALM 46:10

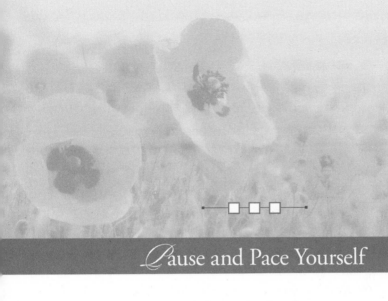

Pause and Pace Yourself

Do not hide your face from your servant;
answer me quickly, for I am in trouble.
—Psalm 69:17

When the walls were crumbling and the floors were falling from beneath him, David called upon God. Can you relate? I can. We wait and wait as our problems fester or our hurts pile up, and then when things explode into chaos or emergencies, we want God to work everything out immediately. When I became sick, I just wanted to get well fast. I thought, *Give me the chemo and radiation, and in a few months I will be back to my usual routine of life.* I didn't mind being sick for a little while, because I knew the doctors and pharmacists had enough skills to solve my problems.

The truth is, God did rescue me—but in His time, not at my hurried pace. After seven long years of treatment there are no signs of cancer in my body. I certainly appreciate God's loving patience.

I often pray for God to keep me humble. Well, He is doing that. I appreciate what God is doing in my life. He has put a strong desire in my soul to spend time every day with Him. I respond, "Let time stand still, and let me forget all about my busy schedule. I want to keep my focus on the Lord."

Prayer: Lord, the world wants You to act swiftly, but I've learned that Your clock moves slower than my watch. Let me learn to adjust to Your timetable. Amen.

Action: Stand in silence for a few minutes. Wait upon the Lord today. Praise Him for His perfect timing in all things.

Today's Wisdom:

Use your trials. What is the purpose of the testing? God makes our trials the instrument of blessing. Too often our trials work impatience, but God will give grace that His real purpose may be accomplished. Patience is more necessary than anything else in our faith life. We forget that time is nothing with God, for with Him a thousand years is as one day, and one day as a thousand years. Christ's purpose in our lives is that we shall be perfect and entire, wanting nothing.

—HENRIETTA MEARS

We Are Called to Be Faithful

I will sing of the LORD's great love forever;
with my mouth I will make your faithfulness
known through all generations.

—PSALM 89:1

The world cries out, "Just be faithful." In all facets of life we hunger for people who will be faithful—in our marriages, with our children, with our churches, with our work, and with our businesses. A faithful person brings peace and harmony to our lives. When we are faithful, we bring peace and harmony to our own lives and to the lives of others.

In Deuteronomy 1 Moses revealed how God had been faithful to him. This is what he shared regarding God's faithfulness to him:

- vv. 1-18—God has been faithful in the past.
- vv. 19-25—God is dependable—He does what He says.
- vv. 24-46—God is fair and just.
- vv. 26-40—When we were fearful and doubting, God was fair and just.
- vv. 37-40—When we were frustrated and overwhelmed, God was fair and just.

- vv. 41-46—When we were arrogant and defiant, God was fair and just.

Moses confirms this concept of faithfulness in Deuteronomy 7:9, "Know therefore that the Lord your God is God; he is the faithful God, keeping his covenant of love to a thousand generations of those who love him and keep his commands."

All throughout Scripture we are challenged to be faithful in our daily lives. We can be faithful to others because God is faithful to us. (All verses are from the New American Standard Bible.)

- Promises

  "Faithful is He who calls you."—1 Thessalonians 5:24
  "He who promised is faithful."—Hebrews 10:23

- Power

  "(God) does not become weary or tired."—Isaiah 40:28

- Character

  "If we are faithless, He remains faithful; for He cannot deny Himself."
  —2 Timothy 2:13

- Protection

  "The Lord is faithful, and He will strengthen and protect you from the evil one."—2 Thessalonians 3:3

- Provision

  "Just as I have been with Moses, I will be with you; I will not fail you or forsake you."—Joshua 1:5

- Temptation

  "No temptation has overtaken you but such as is common to man; and God is faithful, who will not allow you to be tempted beyond what you are able, but with the temptation will provide the way of escape also, that you will be able to endure it."—1 Corinthians 10:13

- Forgiveness

  "If we confess our sins, He is faithful and righteous to forgive us our sins and to cleanse us from all unrighteousness."—1 John 1:9

- Love

  "God is faithful, through whom you were called into fellowship with His Son, Jesus Christ our Lord."—1 Corinthians 1:9

- Hope

  "This I recall to my mind, therefore I have hope. The LORD's loving-kindnesses indeed never cease, for His compassions never fail. They are new every morning; Great is Your faithfulness."—Lamentations 3:21-23

Faithfulness is a "God thing." How faithful we are as women will determine our destiny. God has been faithful in the past, in the present, and He will be faithful in the future. Because God is faithful, we can also be faithful in every situation of life. No wonder God is looking for faithful women.

Prayer: Father God, grant me the desire to be faithful to You. Your Word has made me realize that faithfulness is a great character trait. Give me strength to make daily decisions that will give me life, not death. Because You are faithful, You give me hope for the future. Amen.

Action: Read chapter 1 of Deuteronomy to see how Moses realized God's faithfulness to the Israelites.

Today's Wisdom:

> I've been driven many times to my knees by the overwhelming conviction that I had nowhere else to go.
>
> —ABRAHAM LINCOLN

Put on the New

Now choose life, so that you and your children may live.
—DEUTERONOMY 30:19

Life is a strange journey. We have a choice to make: we choose either life or death. It's that basic. Not too much mental power is needed to figure this formula out. "If anyone is in Christ, he is a new creation; the old has gone, the new has come!" (2 Corinthians 5:17).

What are these old things? They are the natural inclinations that men and women are born with—humanity with all its sinful nature, those things that we need to flee from. In Colossians 3:5-9 it reads:

> So put to death the sinful, earthly things lurking within you. Have nothing to do with sexual immorality, impurity, lust, and evil desires. Don't be greedy, for a greedy person is an idolater, worshiping the things of this world. Because of these sins, the anger of God is coming. You used to do these things when your life was still part of this world. But now is the time to get rid of anger, rage, malicious behavior, slander, and dirty language. Don't lie to each other, for you have stripped off your old sinful nature and all its wicked deeds (NLT).

These are the things we need to put off:

- anger
- rage
- malicious behavior
- slander
- dirty language
- lying

Gee, do I have to give up all of these? Some I really enjoy. What harm is there in keeping a few? When we choose to keep any one of these, in essence we are choosing death. We must come clean and realize that these putting-off items will eventually pull us away from God. He has a plan that spells out life, and His perfect will for our lives is to run as fast as we can from these death items. It means we will be choosing new friends, telling different jokes, reading different magazines, holding our tongues when we want to scream in anger, and no more gossiping or drinking with the boys until late in the evening. These are all death angels to relationships and particularly our marriages and families.

If not these, what must I put on? What does the new life look like?

> Put on your new nature, and be renewed as you learn to know your Creator and become like him. In this new life, it doesn't matter if you are a Jew or a Gentile, circumcised or uncircumcised, barbaric, uncivilized, slave, or free. Christ is all that matters, and he lives in all of us.
>
> Since God chose you to be holy people he loves, you must clothe yourselves with tenderhearted mercy, kindness, humility, gentleness, and patience. Make allowance for each other's faults, and forgive anyone who offends you. Remember, the Lord forgave you, so you must forgive others. Above all, clothe yourselves with love, which binds us all together in perfect harmony.
>
> —COLOSSIANS 3:10-14 (NLT)

What do we need to put on?

- mercy
- kindness
- humility
- gentleness

- patience
- forgiveness
- love

We must be willing to take those things off that lead to death and to put on those things that give life.

Prayer: Father God, give me the courage and strength to take off those things that will prevent me from being all that You want me to be. I so want to be a woman after Your own heart. Amen.

Action: Write down in your journal what you want to put off. Save some room to list what you're going to do to put them off. Give yourself a deadline for accomplishing each. Then do the same for what you want to put on.

Today's Wisdom:

But the fruit of the Spirit is love, joy, peace, patience, kindness, goodness, faithfulness, gentleness and self-control. Against such things there is no law.

—GALATIANS 5:22-23

There's Love All Around

My soul will be satisfied as with the richest of foods;
with singing lips my mouth will praise you.
—Psalm 63:5

One of the ways I praise the Lord and show my abundant joy toward Him is by using creativity in my home. When guests enter through our front door, I want them to see and feel His presence by feeling welcomed and cared for right away. Think of it—we have the opportunity to fashion our lives and our homes into works of art. What a wonderful goal to create a home—a work of art that says, "There's love all around."

One way I've brought love into my home is through what I call our "love shelf." This is a special area in our home where I display those little creative gifts that have come from friends and family over the years. I update it periodically so there is always something new and interesting to share with others. It's a wonderful way to say, "Your gift means a lot to me!"

Add a creative touch to the everyday. As they say, "Think outside of the box." Be you and discover your tastes. Do your thing even if it's not conventional design or style. In other words, have fun with your home. Add a ribbon around your napkins or tuck a fresh flower in some unexpected place in your home.

Create loving moments in the everyday things you do. Don't stay in the same ol' routine. Make yourself a second cup of coffee or tea and take it outside for a moment of fresh air—while there, look around and call out some of God's creations. Express your gratitude for His presence in all that you see. Consider how you have felt God walking alongside you lately, and ask for even greater awareness in the day ahead. Don't forget to ask God to give you a heart for everybody who comes into your home and shares your life there.

Prayer: Father God, You are the Creator, and I'm the created. Give me the creativity to make my home a warm, cozy refuge. Help me liven up my home and infuse it with a sense of Your love and compassion. May I be inspired today. Amen.

Action: Celebrate His love with creativity today in your home and in your life.

Today's Wisdom:

What Is Home?

A roof to keep out the rain. Four walls to keep out the wind. Floors to keep out the cold. Yes, but home is more than that. It is the laughter of children, the song of a mother, the strength of a father. Warmth of loving hearts, light from happy eyes, kindness, loyalty, comradeship. Home is first school and first church for young ones, where they learn what is right, what is good, and what is kind. Where they go for comfort when they are hurt or sick. Where joy is shared and sorrow eased. Where fathers and mothers are respected and loved. Where children are wanted. Where the simplest food is good enough for kings because it is earned. Where money is not so important as loving-kindness. Where even the teakettle sings from happiness. That is home. God bless it.

—ERNESTINE SCHUMANN-HEINK

Be Willing to Say No!

I urge you, brothers, in view of God's mercy, to offer your bodies
as living sacrifices, holy and pleasing to God—
this is your spiritual act of worship.

—ROMANS 12:1

At some point in our lives, we are inclined to ask, "Who am I, Lord?" We will have those defining moments when we have to draw a line in the sand and make a choice not to go over the line. It might be in our careers, our dating, our business dealings, our marriages. We will be challenged and say, "No, that's going over the line."

If we are true to ourselves, we will admit that those choices have come to us. In the past we may have been true to biblical teachings, and at other times we may have gone a little over the line and wished we hadn't. Ideally, for all of us, we want to stay back of the line. However, if you have stepped over the line in the sand, it's not too late to start over again. Be brave (and it does take bravery) to say, "No, I won't compromise my beliefs." Jerome Hines was such a man.

He enjoyed a 40-year career as a bass soloist with the Metropolitan Opera in New York. Standing six and a half feet tall, he was an imposing man whose deep voice was matched by a deep musical talent. He was a rarity among opera singers—he could perform not only in

Italian and French but in German and Russian as well. He was also a deeply committed Christian who authored his own opera, *I Am the Way,* about the life of Jesus, as well as several books including his autobiography of faith, *This Is My Story, This Is My Song.* Jerome Hines lived out Paul's appeal in Romans 12:1 to offer ourselves as living sacrifices to God.

Hines grew up in Southern California and wanted to sing opera from an early age. Before he became a Christian, his only goal was to find fame and fortune on the stage. He trained and sacrificed throughout his early life. He achieved his dream at age 25 when he joined the Met in 1946, replacing the distinguished soloist Ezio Pinza. He was a star—yet he was surprised to find that stardom was not what he expected. Instead of feeling satisfied and fulfilled, he felt empty.

One day, he attended a concert featuring George Beverly Shea, the longtime soloist for the Billy Graham crusades. Hines was impressed by the power of Shea's voice—a voice that could easily have taken Shea to Broadway or the operatic stage. Hines wondered why Shea had dedicated his life to singing at evangelistic crusades. Listening to George Beverly Shea sing "I'd Rather Have Jesus," Hines was struck by the message of the song emphasized by one line: "I'd rather have Jesus than anything this world affords today."[13]

Listening to those words, Hines realized why his life seemed so empty. He had set his heart on fame and fortune—but only Jesus brings satisfaction and fulfillment. So Jerome Hines turned his life over to the Lord Jesus. As a Christian, Hines continued to sing opera, but now he sang for the glory of God. Years after his conversion, he was placed in a position of having to pay a high price for his decision to live for Christ.

After months of training for an operatic role he had always wanted to sing, he went to a rehearsal. He was shocked to see several performers engaging in a lewd and offensive dance. Hines went to the director and asked, "What are those dancers doing?"

"That," said the director, "is the choreography that introduces the opera."

"But there's no such choreography in this opera!" Hines said. "It has never been performed that way!"

"We're modernizing it," the director said, "bringing it up to date for today's audiences. It'll be a big hit. Audiences love this kind of innovation."

"It's pornographic!" Hines said. "I won't lend my talent to such a lewd performance."

"Well," said the director, "you'll have to talk to Mr. Bing about that."

So Jerome Hines went to Rudolph Bing, the general manager of the Metropolitan Opera Company. After Hines explained his objections, Bing replied, "We have a contract. If you don't sing, you'll never perform again."

"You may break my career," said Hines, "but you won't change my mind. If that dance is in the opera, I will not sing."

Finally, Bing relented—but only partly. "All right, Jerome," Bing said. "I can see you're serious about this. You don't have to sing—but the opera will go on as planned, including the dance. We'll just have to put another singer in the role."

So Jerome Hines gave up the role he had dreamed of—a decision that cost him at least a hundred thousand dollars. But Jerome Hines remained faithful to his Lord. At considerable cost to himself, he had offered his body and his voice as a living sacrifice, holy and pleasing to God.[14]

Prayer: Father God, You are a God of principle. I don't want to pay the price of living if it has little value. Give me the courage to be brave in my life. Amen.

Action: Take a close look at what you haven't yet given over to God for Him to shape. Examine your family, career, dreams, home, relationships, hobbies, and anything else that is part of your life.

Today's Wisdom:

If I can right a human wrong,
If I can help to make one strong,
If I can cheer with smile or song,
Lord, show me how.

—GRENVILLE KLEISER

Full and Overflowing with Joy

You have made known to me the path of life;
you will fill me with joy in your presence,
with eternal pleasures at your right hand.
—Psalm 16:11

The joy of the Lord is much broader, much larger, much deeper, much more lasting than everyday happiness. When our joy flows from a heart transformed by Christ, we are responding to the wonder of being loved completely by God. When we have the joy of the Lord, we can be glad for a new day, a new sunset, a new baby, a new season, a new ending, a new beginning, a new chance, and even a new trial. We are able to rejoice when we have the joy of the Lord.

When Mother Teresa was asked what the job description was for anyone who might wish to work alongside her in the dirty streets of India among the death and devastation of the highly populated city of Calcutta, she responded "The desire to work hard and a joyful attitude."

I would say this is also a formula for real success. No matter what is on our plates for the day, God calls us to labor over it with joy. We are serving Him when we clean the house, prepare for a meeting, visit a friend, or take care of our parents or our children. Have you ever noticed that those who have a lot of friends are those who work hard and are able to do so with joy? They impact everyone around them. Adopting God's heart for all you do and for everyone you meet gives you that quality. When I feel down, I want to exhibit joyfulness, and when I feel lazy, I want a new zeal in my body. This comes from the Lord.

Frank C. Laubach stated it very nicely when he wrote, "Your joy comes from what you give, not from what you accumulate." The richest person leaves everything when she dies. Only her joy will be a living legacy for those who are left behind.

Prayer: Father God, I want to live a life that experiences more than daily happiness or contentment that rises and falls with my moods. Lead me to experience and express Your joy. My heart yearns to be full of joy reflecting Your love in my life. Amen.

Action: Lift your heart and your spirits today by expressing joy. Sing. Dance. Draw. Pray. Laugh. Share. Find a way to show that joy!

Today's Wisdom:

All sorts of things can undermine happiness—time, change, and tragedy above all. There isn't anything intrinsically wrong with happiness, but waiting for just the right circumstances or the ideal situation in order to be happy will keep you from fully living your life and experiencing God's joy.

But the answer is not to reject happiness, it is to go beyond it, to joy.... Rooted in God, empowered by the energies of the resurrection, joy does not depend on getting the right income, the perfect spouse, the right mix of things. Joy goes so far beyond happiness that it is present even in the midst of deep unhappiness.

—REBECCA M. PIPPERT

The Whys and the Wise

We know that in all things God works for the good of those who love him,
who have been called according to his purpose.
—ROMANS 8:28

Have you ever asked the question "Why me, Lord?" When I was first diagnosed with cancer, I had all kinds of questions cross my mind. However, from past difficult situations I knew that nothing came to us before it first came through God. Without a doubt our family knew that all things work together for good. The secular world doesn't know or understand that principle. As believers, we can be at peace when trials come our way. We can know that we are not alone in that trial.

Are you one who wallows in the whys of life? Or are you wise in the Lord? Faith and time in God's Word gives us a wisdom that surpasses any knowledge or wisdom we could gain on our own even if we lived a hundred years. Have you ever watched one of your children struggle with something that seemed simple to you but was very complex and confusing to him? Your wisdom and experience can see through the trouble to the solution. His limited encounter with problems keeps him from seeing past what feels like an insurmountable barrier. God's wisdom is just like that…it sees the clear path to the solution when we are struggling to see anything with our very human, limited view.

Many times we wonder why God would let us go through such bad and difficult times. But God knows that when He puts these things all in His order, they always work for good. We just have to trust Him, and eventually, they will all make something wonderful!

Prayer: Father God, give me Your clarity in my current life situation. When I am struggling or face a trial, keep me from drowning in the whys so that I can become wise in You. Amen.

Action: Give your trouble over to God today. Give it to His wisdom, and see what He wants to make of your trial. Prepare to be amazed.

Today's Wisdom:

Learn wisdom from the ways of a seedling. A seedling which is never hardened off through stressful situations will never become a strong productive plant.

—Stephen Sigmund

In Search of the Rock

Lead me to the rock that is higher than I.
—Psalm 61:2

All of us are looking for a rock to stand on, a solid foundation that will give us the hope and securities of life. But so often we place ourselves on the wrong foundation and then wonder why there is no comfort, strength, or grace to be found. As Joshua proclaimed to his family in his latter years, "If serving the LORD seems undesirable to you, then choose for yourselves this day whom you will serve, whether the gods your forefathers served beyond the River, or the gods of the Amorites, in whose land you are living. But as for me and my household, we will serve the LORD" (Joshua 24:15).

It was clear that Joshua had found his rock of protection, security, comfort—and it was the God of Israel.

There is a story about two small roads that ran side by side. They chatted as they wound in and out of country places, laughing with the brook, sighing with the wind, and resting now and then along the level knolls. There they watched the trees put on their green gloves in springtime, raise their leafy umbrellas for summer shade, wind tawny shawls around their shoulders in autumn, and lace their limbs with snowflakes when winter came.

They were very happy little roads because they did their jobs well. School children walked upon them and wagons rolled smoothly upon them. Shy little creatures played games along their ruts when nobody was near. On and on they went until at last they came to a little incline. One road panted at the effort, but the other road encouraged it to come along. The hill eventually grew steeper, and the tired road said, "I can't make it. I'm going back." The other road worked very hard and grew very weary, but at last it came to the summit and danced over the world beyond.

As we travel through life, most of what we encounter is pretty easy. But when we occasionally reach the steep hills, we come to a screeching halt. These hills seem to be barriers to our dreams and wishes about life. We're tempted to turn back because we become tired and can't imagine making the steep climb to the top of the hill.

But the mother who faces such challenges, the woman who can discipline her life through the hardships and setbacks, will soon sail over the summit of the hill and down the other side into the glorious Valley of Victory. We all have choices to make; we come to a fork in the road, and we must make a choice. Joshua had the same opportunity to make his choice, and he chose the Lord God of Israel to be his rock. We all are given the same opportunity. Which choice are you making?

Prayer: Father God, give me the strength to finish the race set before me. Give me abundant endurance to follow You all the days of my life. Amen.

Action: Strengthen your walking muscles so that you can climb steep hills. A good brisk or even leisurely walk is a great break from a trying day.

Today's Wisdom:

In the hour of adversity be not without hope
For crystal rain falls from black clouds.

—Nizami

Mysteries of Life

Pray also for me, that whenever I open my mouth,
words may be given me so that I will fearlessly make known
the mystery of the gospel.
—Ephesians 6:19

The more I study Scripture, the more I encounter mysteries that I can't understand. All of these are beyond my human understanding. I ponder, but they still are classified as unfathomable by my simple mind. However, there are also some everyday mysteries I must ponder. Here is a list I ran across that reveals the quirky mysteries of our everyday life, such as:

- Can you cry under water?
- How important does a person have to be before he's considered assassinated instead of just murdered?
- If money doesn't grow on trees, why do banks have branches?
- Since bread is square, then why is sandwich meat round?
- Why do you have to "put your two cents in"…but it's only a penny for your thoughts. Where's that extra penny going to?
- What did cured ham actually have?

- How is it that we put a man on the moon before we figured out it would be a good idea to put wheels on luggage?
- Why is it that people say they "slept like a baby" when babies wake up every two hours?
- Why are you IN a movie, but you're ON TV?
- Why do people pay to go up tall buildings and then put money in binoculars to look at things on the ground?
- How come we choose from just two people for president and 50 for Miss America?
- If a 911 operator has a heart attack, whom does he/she call?
- Why is "bra" singular and "panties" plural?
- The hardest thing to learn in life is which bridge to cross and which to burn.
- What do you call a male ladybug?[15]

These are humorous ponderings, but the faith life presents much more serious ponderings; for example: Will we ever understand the mystery and wonder of God's forgiveness and love of sinful creatures? Only by God's grace can this happen. As sinners, we become white as snow. Our minds are not big enough to understand all of His mysteries. I leave God's secrets to Him.

From an old church hymn, I rest on His promise: "Only Believe."

> Fear not, little flock, from the cross to the throne
> From death into life He went for His own;
> All power in earth, all power above,
> Is given to Him for the flock of His love.
>
> Chorus:
>
> Only believe, only believe;
> All things are possible, only believe,
> Only believe, only believe;
> All things are possible, only believe.
>
> —Paul Rader

When we believe, the pondering of these mysteries of Scripture ceases to be so important. We trust and believe that God is in charge of these big issues, and we only have to worry about the simple things here on earth. I'm glad to bow down before Him and give Him all my trust on the big mysteries.

Prayer: Father God, let me not get bogged down with the mysteries in Scripture. Let me be assured that You have inspired all Scripture. Let me put my trust 100 percent in Your handling of these mysteries. Amen.

Action: Write down in your journal any mysteries you are pondering. Give time for you to resolve these questions. Date them when and if they are answered. Don't become impatient with God's timing.

Today's Wisdom:

Knowledge is horizontal. Wisdom is vertical—it comes down from above.

—BILLY GRAHAM

Less Is Best

Commit your way to the LORD;
trust in him and he will do this.
—PSALM 37:5

When we commit our ways to the Lord, He will direct our paths. One of the paths on which He will direct us is that of organization. Since God created all things in an orderly fashion, He wants us to have organization and order in our homes.

Caring for our homes brings a great feeling of accomplishment. Our belongings will last longer and those unexpected drop-in visitors will not send us scurrying around to tidy up our disorder. We'll feel relaxed when family and guests arrive unexpectedly.

I have found that when you have a mess surrounding you in your physical environment and that mess remains over time, it holds you at your current level of effectiveness. For example, when you are overwhelmed, you can't see anything else. You can't see new opportunities, challenges, or even how to care for someone else. You protest, "Are you kidding? I've got too much to handle already. I'm about ready to lose my cool."

The messes in your home many times reflect messes in your personal life. I honestly believe that if you don't know what you want out of life, it's hard to prioritize the activities of your life. Taking the time to establish goals for your life is very basic to helping you clean out the messes that prevent you from doing the things you want to do but don't have time to do. Are you content with who you are?

Thomas Fuller says, "Contentment consists not in adding more fuel, but in taking away some fire; not in multiplying of wealth, but in subtracting men's desires." I have a personal motto for my life: "Less is best."

When you don't have something, you don't have to dust it, paint it, repair it, or replace it. When we are young, we strive to consume; as we get older, we try to cut back and eliminate possessions from our lives that rob us of being content. If we can't find contentment within ourselves, it is useless to seek it elsewhere. Each person chooses to be content or discontent. Which will it be? Whichever option you choose will determine if you are ready to eliminate the messes and clutter from your life, home, and work.

Prayer: Father God, since You are a God of order, I want my life to reflect Your character. Give me a contentment about my station in life. Amen.

Action: Choose one area of one room to organize today. Have fun with the process.

Today's Wisdom:

If you aren't content with what you have, you will never be content with what you want.

There's Always a "But..."

We know that in all things God works for the good of those who love him,
who have been called according to his purpose.
—ROMANS 8:28

I've noticed in Scripture that with many promises there is a condition attached. In this key verse of evangelical Christians, we read and believe that all things do work together for good—in our own families we believe that because God says it and we have experienced it in our own lives. However, for this to be true, we must meet a condition. That being:

to those who love him,
who have been called according to his purpose.

This promise is reserved for the children of God. Sometimes this promise is given to an unbeliever in order to give her comfort after the death of a loved one, a bad outcome in business, or even a failed marriage. When we use this verse improperly, it may give comfort, but this promise is only for the believer who has been chosen by God to be one of His children.

This verse is also a test of our loyalty to God. Are we only fair-weather Christians? Or can we remain loyal to God even during the difficult times of our lives? As Job was being tested by God, his wife asked him this question, "Do you still hold fast your integrity? Curse God and die!" Job's faithful response was classic: "Shall we indeed accept good from God and not accept adversity?" (Job 2:9-10 NASB).

Can we still see God's purpose for us in times of illness, death, lack of food, lack of work, lack of money, lack of home, and lack of family?

In our culture we are challenged to remain loyal to our work, our sports teams, our country, our schools, our spouses, and our children, but seldom are we encouraged to remain loyal to God through all situations.

Larry Crabb reminds his readers in *The Marriage Builder* that the hope of the Christian lies not in a change of circumstances, which God may or may not bring about, but in the grace of God. We aren't to hope that the circumstances will change, but we are to hope in God's grace—in His unearned, undeserved, and unconditional love for us.

God promises to permit only those events to enter our lives that will further His purpose in our lives. Our responsibility is to respond to life's events in a way that will please the Lord, and not to try to change the circumstances into what we want.[16]

The idea is not that we work for God, but because of our loyalty to Him, He can work through us. Remember that God is the Potter, and we are the clay. He wants to conform us to His own image, not our image. Since Americans exist in a "live for now and feel good" culture, this fact is hard to live out. We only want to do things that feel good and serve an immediate need or want. Many of life's character-building circumstances don't feel good. In fact, they often are quite painful. They are events that we wouldn't choose for ourselves.

As a woman, reaffirm your loyalty to God today. Acknowledge that He is God and that He only permits those events to come into your life that are life-forming for you.

Prayer: Father God, I want to be loyal to You and trust that all things work together for good. This is a renewed trust. Give me the courage to live it out in my life. Amen.

Action: Acknowledge that everything you have is on loan from God. He is the Potter and you are the clay. Let Him mold you in His own way.

Today's Wisdom:

> I will repay you for the years the locusts have eaten—
>> the great locust and the young locust,
>> the other locusts and the locust swarm—
> my great army that I sent among you.
>
> —JOEL 2:25

Searching for Love and Wisdom

Where can wisdom be found?
Where does understanding dwell?
—Job 28:12

We tend to look for love in all the wrong places—we seek wisdom in places where there is a greater chance of encountering gossip, bad advice, or false truths than there is of encountering godly wisdom. We live in a culture that wants to bypass true wisdom. We want shortcuts to a deeper understanding of life and purpose before we go to the Father's feet and ask for such direction.

The writer of the book of Job struggled with knowing what to do. In Job 28:12 he asked, "Where can wisdom be found?" All through chapter 28 he searched for the answer:

- Mankind doesn't know its value (v. 13).
- It is not found in the land of the living (v. 13).
- The inner earth says, "It's not in me" (v. 14).
- The sea says, "It's not in me" (v. 14).
- You can't buy it with gold or silver (v. 15).
- Precious stones don't have it (v. 16).

- It can't be equated with gold (v. 17).
- Pearls don't have it (v. 18).
- It is hidden from the eyes of all living creatures (v. 21).
- God understands its way, and He knows its place (v. 23).
- God looks to the ends of the earth and sees everything under heaven (v. 24).
- God saw wisdom and declared it (v. 27).
- God established it and searched it out (v. 27).

Job and his friends claimed wisdom of themselves, but wisdom is clearly an outgrowth of God and not merely something to be obtained. Although we can know and understand many things, we cannot attain the level of Creator wisdom. There will always be questions that only God can answer. Solomon knew that true wisdom is not found in human understanding but is from God alone (see Proverbs 1:7).

If you are searching for truth and direction and wisdom to raise your family, choose your career, make a big decision, or step forward in your life in some way, then it is time to seek God's Word and His guidance through prayer and faithfulness. Don't look where there is not truth but only more confusion. Even our best friends can add more opinions to our decision making but not necessarily truth and clarity. When you face a fork in the road, spend time waiting for God to direct your next step.

Prayer: Father God, I come before You seeking Your knowledge and direction for my life. When I want the fast answer instead of waiting for Your wisdom, grant me patience. Help me hold out for nothing short of Your absolute truth. Amen.

Action: Search your heart today for some answers. A heart

given over to God holds amazing truth. Take time to listen.

Today's Wisdom:

God is crazy about you. He sends you flowers every spring and a sunrise every morning. Whenever you want to talk, He'll listen. He can live anywhere in the universe, and He chose your heart.

—AUTHOR UNKNOWN

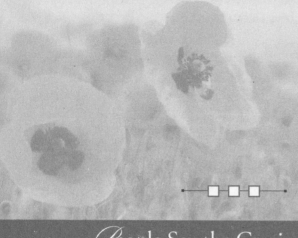

People Say the Craziest Things

Everything is funny as long as it happens to someone else.
—WILL ROGERS

We live in an age of constant communication. A slip of the tongue or of the pen can certainly change what we meant to say. We know what we mean, but it doesn't always come out that way.

The following are actual announcements (including misprints) taken from church bulletins. If you have been associated with churches over any length of time, you will be able to decode them and know what the writer had in mind.

- Don't let worry kill you. Let the church help.

- Thursday night potluck supper. Prayer and medication to follow.

- Remember in prayer the many who are sick of our church and community.

- For those of you who have children and don't know it, we have a nursery downstairs.

- The rosebud on the altar this morning is to announce the birth of David Alan Belzer, the sin of Rev. and Mrs. Julius Belzer.

- This afternoon there will be a meeting in the south and north ends of the church. Children will be baptized at both ends.

- At the evening service tonight, the sermon topic will be "What Is Hell?" Come early and listen to our choir practice.

- Weight Watchers will meet at 8 P.M. at the First Presbyterian Church. Please use large double doors at the side entrance.

- Eight new choir robes are currently needed, due to the addition of several new members and the deterioration of some older ones.

- The Senior Choir invites any member of the congregation who enjoys sinning to join the choir.

- Scouts are saving aluminum cans, bottles and other items to be recycled. Proceeds will be used to cripple children.[17]

We occasionally need a good laugh, and we always need a good sense of humor. Share some of these with your fellow workers today. It's so good to be able to laugh at ourselves. After all, the Bible says we are to be joyful people.

Prayer: Father God, since You are the Creator of mankind, You must have a good sense of humor, because a lot of us are so funny. Thanks for letting me take time to laugh. Amen.

Action: Buy a joke book and read a joke or two a day. We all need to stop taking life so seriously.

Today's Wisdom:
Those who bring sunshine to the lives of others cannot keep it from themselves.

—JAMES M. BARRIE

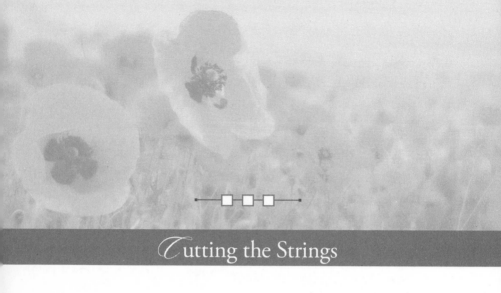

Cutting the Strings

Delight yourself in the LORD
and he will give you the desires of your heart.
—Psalm 37:4

As parents we have many desires for our children. One is that they will grow into well-adjusted, responsible adults. Along the way we have a tendency to overprotect them in an effort to keep them from the bruises of life. It isn't easy to see them hurt, disappointed, or crying, but those things must be experienced in their youth or they will not know how to handle them as adults. Cutting the cord is very difficult. If we have the desire to lead children to independence, we must cut that cord. If we don't, we run the risk of hurting or impeding children who eventually must face adulthood—prepared or not prepared.

The hardest experience most women will ever face is "letting go" of their children. The empty nest phase of life is difficult and at times very lonely. But in order for each party to have healthy tomorrows we must let go. It doesn't mean that we are no longer available to our children (in fact, many times we are closer). We might not have the parent-child relationship, but we can enjoy and strengthen the evolving relationship between two adults. You might be years away from this transition, but know that it can be such a great joy to have that adult friendship with a daughter or son. Don't fear that change, instead look forward to it. Don't mourn your children's birthdays because they mean that they are growing up too fast for your liking; instead, prepare for new wonders for your life and the lives of your children. Open your arms to the new desires God has for you up ahead—desires beyond what you could ever imagine. Be willing to dream bigger than you ever thought possible.

Cutting the apron strings might not be easy, but I know that with God's help you and I can cut the strings and see how God gives us new desires to fill, satisfy, and inspire us.

Prayer: Father God, You know how difficult it is to let go of anything, let alone my children. With Your help I know I can do it. Help me to place them in Your care through prayer and to encourage them in their faith and future. Amen.

Action: List in your journal three desires you have for your child's future. List three desires that you have for your future.

Today's Wisdom:

The character and history of each child may be a new and poetic experience to the parent, if he will let it.

—MARGARET FULLER

Be Strong When You Are Weak

I will extol the LORD at all times;
his praise will always be on my lips.
—Psalm 34:1

On November 8, 1994, Scott and Janet Willis and six of their children were traveling on Interstate Highway 94 when a bracket fell from a truck and punctured their minivan's gas tank, causing a fire and explosion that instantly claimed the lives of five of their children, and caused the eventual death of a sixth child. Janet and Scott escaped only because they were sitting in the front of the van where the flames could not engulf them as quickly.

As the story circled the media, anyone listening to their faith in God, their intense love for their children, and their grace-filled compassion toward the truck driver had to be moved by this extraordinary couple. As I prayed for their situation, I kept remembering Janet's gentle, peaceful face. Sit down with us as this humble woman shares some of her thoughts.

> The children and I were sleeping in the van when the accident occurred. Scott told me to get out of the car. In order to do that, I had to dip my hands into a roaring

fire to unlatch my safety belt. I then fell out the door while the car was still moving. Everything was wild! I ended up on the side of the road screaming, "No God, not my children, no, no, no!" Scott got to me and said, "It was quick. They are with the Lord. Janet, this is what we have been prepared for."

I realized I had been saying, "no, no, no," to God as my children were entering heaven's door. I was saying, "no, God" to the very thing I ultimately wanted most for our children—to be with God eternally. I forced myself to repeat Psalm 34:1, "I will bless the LORD at all times."

God had been preparing them for this time. All of the lessons, all the preparation, all the promises, all the spiritual fiber He had woven into them has held Scott and Janet Willis together.

Janet said, "We have thrown ourselves into God's grace."[18]

What a wonderful example of unfailing faith. Scott and Janet have captured the complete essence of the Christian life. They understand why we are placed on this earth. As Paul knew when he wrote to the church at Corinth, "'My grace is sufficient for you, for my power is made perfect in weakness'...For when I am weak, then I am strong" (2 Corinthians 12:9-10).

Oh, if we in the church today could only grasp the concept that Christ's grace is sufficient and it's all that we need in *every* situation. There is great peace in acknowledging and accepting the sufficiency of God's grace by allowing Him to be strong during our periods of weaknesses. As human beings, we want to be strong at all times and not allow Him to be strong for us when we are weak. He is all we need.

Prayer: Father God, thank You for giving this story that models how I want to live out my walk with You. Prepare me *now* so I can respond likewise *then*. Thank You for being there when I am weak. Amen.

Action: Thank God every day for the health and safety of your family.

Today's Wisdom:

> I said a prayer for you today,
> And know God must have heard,
> I felt the answer in my heart,
> Although He spoke no word....
> I asked that He'd be near you,
> At the start of each new day,
> To grant you health and blessings,
> And friends to share your way.
> I asked for happiness for you
> In all things great and small,
> But it was for His loving care
> I prayed the most of all.

> —MARGARET GOULD

*G*rateful Living

Praise be to the LORD,
for he has heard my cry for mercy.
—Psalm 28:6

*W*hen we are in distress, we quickly plead with God to hear our wishes: "Give me this, don't let that happen, protect me from harm, heal me from sickness, watch over my sick child..." Is your list as endless as mine? We ask God for all kinds of miracles, but do we ever take time to thank Him for His presence, for His answers to those requests? We teach our children to say thank you when they are very young, but we often forget to say the same magic words when God so graciously gives us something.

This is the perfect reason for us to record our prayer requests. When they are written down in a notebook or journal, we then have a place to write down the answers we receive. Do you assume you'll remember? Take a moment to think back over just this past year. I'll bet there are countless prayers God answered that you had already forgotten. So pull out the pen and paper and write down your requests. Later you can reflect back on the many reasons you have to praise the Lord and to thank Him.

There will still be times when you are waiting for your answer or hoping for a different answer, but when you trust in God's plan and purpose for you, you can lift up your thanks no matter what, because You know He has you in the palm of His hand and cares deeply about you and your life.

We should be quick to show our appreciation because our heavenly Father is pleased when we thank Him. I know I was pleased as a mom when I would hear my children tell someone thank you without my having to remind them to do so.

When our Lord was on earth, He lifted His voice to His Father and expressed thanks for food (see John 6:11), the simplicity of the gospel (see Matthew 11:25), and answered prayer (see John 11:41). What do you have to be grateful for? Say those precious words "thank you" and give God glory for all He has done.

Prayer: Father God, as a mother, I love to hear "thank you"; so I know You must also want to hear from us when You so graciously hear and answer our supplications.

Action: Thank God today in a special way. Say it by serving one of His children or by journaling a note of gratitude. Praise Him all day for His faithfulness.

Today's Wisdom:

In the end we shall find every promise of God perfectly fulfilled. Then why should we not let our hearts rest in peace about everything that happens? Nothing can happen that can break a single one of these precious promises. There is no promise of an easy passage, but there are promises for every day of the voyage. Each day let us take one promise for our own, live on it, test and prove it—and thank God for it.

—Amy Carmichael

*P*lay and Praise

Rejoice in the LORD and be glad, you righteous;
sing, all you who are upright in heart!
—Psalm 32:11

There's nothing like seeing a yard full of young children. They let out all the stops—no inhibition in those young bodies. I think Jesus loved young children so much because of their innocence and their ability to let loose with joy. Now that our children are grown, we get to experience the joy of our grandchildren who live near. What we have found over the years, surrounded by children and their laughter and energy, is that when we take time to play, we are taking time to praise God with our delight.

It's so simple to delight a child. Use your imagination, and you'll tap into your own sense of wonder and delight. Try these ideas and see if they help you become more joyful and content. They will definitely help you connect with the children in your life!

Children love to pretend, imagine, and create. Around our home, we have created toy centers—places where the grandchildren can congregate and find lots of things to entertain and amuse themselves. One of these centers is upstairs in a loft. This is where Granny stores all her old vintage clothes. The kids love to dress up with old dresses, scarves, necklaces, gloves, and high-heel shoes. Some of our most memorable photographs are of the grandchildren dressed for their fancy tea parties. Even the boys will fit into PaPa's old contributions. Another toy center is in our breakfast area. There we have a large trunk full of blocks, railroad tracks, locomotives, and Tonka trucks. Occasionally the girls are here, but this is really the boys' hangout.

In the toy center you create, be sure to include the best element of all, a fabric-covered box that each child knows is his or her own. It's always there, ready for play. Inside the box are quiet activities to amuse children who might come with Mom for a visit: crayons, coloring books, blank pieces of drawing paper, and a few simple games.

In my pantry and refrigerator, I designate an area for child-friendly snacks, juice, peanut butter, and fruit wraps. It doesn't take much to make your home child-friendly and play-ready. Think of the dividends it will bring to you and your children. You'll find that your children's friends will love to visit. And all this play is infectious. You might start thinking of things to put in your own toy center...good books to read, drawing pens and a sketch pad, a devotional, a book of humorous stories, a magazine...the ideas are endless.

Prayer: Father God, restore unto me a childlike heart. You have given me everything I need for life and godliness. Let me enter each day with abundance and joy. Amen.

Action: Create several toy centers for the children in your home.

Today's Wisdom:

What families have in common the world around is that they are the place where people learn who they are and how to be that way.

—JEAN ILLSLEY CLARKE

Stop Struggling with Your Problems

Wait for the LORD;
be strong, and let your heart take courage;
yes wait for the LORD.
—Psalm 27:14 NASB

We continually find ourselves fighting to stay in control. We think that if we're in control, we'll be capable of resolving our own struggles. And there are many times that we think we'd do a much better job than God is doing. We are so impatient, aren't we? Scripture tells us to wait on the Lord. His clock ticks at a different pace than our watches. When we want to hurry—God often says wait.

"Be merciful to me, LORD, for I am faint; O LORD, heal me, for my bones are in agony" (Psalm 6:2). In this psalm, David is asking God how long his suffering will last. Do you have a trial that seems insurmountable? Are you walking alongside a friend who faces pain or illness? Is your family dealing with addiction or another affliction that presents a constant source of struggle? Then you know what it is to cry out to God for relief, for mercy, and for healing.

I uttered the same pleas when my doctor announced that I had cancer. Little did I realize how sick I would become or how long the road ahead of me would be. There were moments when I didn't think

I would live another day. During this time of uncertainty, my Bob and I asked God countless times a day to deliver me from the prison of illness. At times it didn't seem like He was even listening to our pleas. Often we were discouraged, but we hung our faith on the character of God and all of His promises. I didn't know then that someday I would have the quality of life that I have today.

I will be honest with you…you and I will never fully understand how God works, and we most certainly will not understand His timeline. But what we are supposed to learn through all these experiences is how to wait upon the Lord and wait for the Lord's grace, strength, peace, and direction. Are you waiting upon the Lord for an answer, for reprieve, for help? He has heard your cries and is answering them.

Prayer: Father God, why do I look to the left and to the right when I need to look up to find the answers to life's difficulties? Teach me to go to You directly and to stop looking in all the wrong places. Amen.

Action: Pray for the specifics of your situation, but be willing to let go of the timeline to God's plan.

Today's Wisdom:

One of the most tragic things I know about human nature is that all of us tend to put off living. We are all dreaming of some magical rose garden over the horizon—instead of enjoying the roses that are blooming outside our window today.

—DALE CARNEGIE

Do not fear, for I am with you;
do not anxiously look about you,
for I am your God.
I will strengthen you,
surely I will help you,
surely I will uphold you
with My righteous right hand.

—ISAIAH 41:10 NASB

Who I Am in Christ

To all who received him, to those who believed in his name,
he gave the right to become children of God.
—John 1:12

Many of us worry about how others perceive us, so rather than rest in who we are, we pursue achievement, success, or status no matter what sacrifice is involved. Those sacrifices start to undermine our life's value and our satisfaction, so the cycle begins again…and we find ourselves allowing our personal worth to be determined by what our family, friends, teachers, neighbors, pastors, or others think about us.

Who am I? This is a basic question we face in life. And for the answer, we can either look to what others think of us as truth, or we can discover who God says we are. Others' opinions are short-lived and will soon pass away, but God's thoughts are eternal and will be everlasting. So which will you fully trust?

Nothing is more freeing than agreeing with God about how He sees you and me. That's why it is so important to be in a daily study of God's Word. This exercise will offer us several key pieces of information.

- We will know who God is.

- We will know who we are in Him.
- We will know what we have in Him.
- We will know what we can do through Him.

Day by day we are to live out who we are as new creations in Christ Jesus. The following alphabet is just the beginning of our relationship with God the Father, God the Son, and God the Holy Spirit.

Able to do all things—Philippians 4:13

Becoming conformed to Christ—Romans 8:29

Chosen—Colossians 3:12

Delivered—2 Timothy 4:18

Equipped—2 Timothy 3:17

Filled with joy—John 17:13

Guarded by God—2 Timothy 1:12

Holy—Hebrews 10:10

Instrument of righteousness—Romans 6:13

Justified—1 Corinthians 6:11

Known—2 Timothy 2:19

Lacking no wisdom—James 1:5

Made by Him—Psalm 100:3

Never forsaken—Philippians 4:19

Overcomer—1 John 5:4-5

Partaker of grace—Philippians 1:7

Qualified to share His inheritance—Colossians 1:12

Received the riches of grace—Ephesians 1:7

Sealed by God with the Holy Spirit—Ephesians 1:13

Transformed in His image—2 Corinthians 3:18

Useful for His glory—Isaiah 43:7

Valued—Matthew 6:26

Walking in new life—Romans 6:4

E**X**ample—Ephesians 5:2

Yielded to God—Romans 6:13

Zeal for God—Romans 6:13

Just think of all the value we have in Christ. His Word says that I'm important and I have worth in His eyes. No matter what others may think of me, I have eternal value.

- I am deeply loved.
- I am complete in Him.
- He made me special.
- He made me beautiful in His sight.
- I am pleasing to Him.
- I am forgiven in Him.
- He wants to have fellowship with me.

Prayer: Father God, no matter what I think of myself, Your Word tells me that I'm more valuable than gold or silver. As I look in the mirror, may I see Your face reflecting back to me. Thank You for loving me so much. Amen.

Action: Each day go through the ABC's of who you are and study the reference Scriptures.

Today's Wisdom:

On the whole, God's love for us is a much safer subject to think about than our love for him. Nobody can always have devout feelings; and even if we could, feelings are not what God principally cares about. Christian love, either toward God or toward man, is an affair of the will. But the great thing to remember is that, though our feelings come and go, his love for us does not.

—C.S. Lewis

There Will Be Storms in Life

A righteous man may have many troubles,
but the LORD delivers him from them all.
—Psalm 34:19

Never in the history of America have we had such assault on our country in the form of hurricanes. Bob and I just experienced such a storm while we were doing a seminar in Jacksonville, Florida. We were able to catch the last plane out before a hurricane hit the Florida coast. If we had not caught that plane, we would have been reluctant captives for three days as this area was hit by a destructive storm.

When we got home, we turned on our TV to catch up on the latest news. We grieved with those who had lost loved ones, businesses, homes, cars, and contents of their homes. The cleanup process was horrendous and would require much money and effort. We realized that millions of lives will never be the same.

Many of us are experiencing storms that are as devastating as these tragedies of nature. They are not as evident as a hurricane, but they are just as real and as difficult to overcome. These storms can turn our dreams into hellish nightmares. They're called: divorce, disease, death, betrayal, bankruptcy, ill health, abuse, adultery, addiction.... Such storms have devastated individuals and families.

What do we do when storms hit our lives? Do we go to the newsstand and find a book or magazine that will help us get through them? In the first place you won't find your answer at the newsstand. For me and my family, we will look to Scripture to see what God has to say (All Scriptures are from the New American Standard Bible):

- God has a purpose for our lives.

  "We know that God causes all things to work together for good to those who love God, to those who are called according to His purpose."—Romans 8:28

  "All Scripture is inspired by God and profitable for teaching, for reproof; for correction, for training in righteousness; so that the man of God may be adequate, equipped for every good work." —2 Timothy 3:16-17

- God is praying for us and protecting us.

  "He is able also to save forever those who draw near to God through Him, since He always lives to make intercession for them." —Hebrews 7:25

  "The LORD is near to all who call upon Him…in truth."—Psalm 145:18

  "We do not know how to pray as we should, but the Spirit Himself intercedes for us with groanings too deep for words."—Romans 8:26

  "Therefore, let everyone who is godly pray to You in a time when You may be found."—Psalm 32:6

  "You are my hiding place; You preserve me from trouble; You surround me with songs of deliverance."—Psalm 32:7-8

  "Everyone who asks receives, and he who seeks finds, and to him who knocks it will be opened."—Matthew 7:8

  "All things you ask in prayer, believing, you will receive."—Matthew 21:22

- We have God's presence.

In each of these Scriptures we read that Jesus was present through each person's storm. He did not leave them alone. In all our storms of life He is always with us.

"My presence shall go with you, and I will give you rest."—Exodus 33:14

"Be strong and courageous! Do not tremble or be dismayed, for the LORD your God is with you wherever you go."—Joshua 1:9

"I will never desert you, nor will I ever forsake you."—Hebrews 13:5

- We have the peace of God.

   "In my distress I called upon the LORD, and cried to my God for help; He heard my voice out of His temple, and my cry for help before Him came into His ears."—Psalm 18:6

   "Why are you troubled, and why do doubts arise in your hearts." —Luke 24:38

   "Peace I leave with you; My peace I give to you; not as the world gives do I give to you. Do not let your heart be troubled, nor let it be fearful."—John 14:27

   "He Himself is our peace."—Ephesians 2:14

- We have God's power.

   "You will receive power when the Holy Spirit has come upon you." —Acts 1:8

   " 'My grace is sufficient for you, for power is perfected in weakness.' Most gladly, therefore, I will rather boast about my weaknesses, so that the power of Christ may dwell in me."—2 Corinthians 12:9

   "God has not given us a spirit of timidity, but of power and love and discipline."—2 Timothy 1:7

These five truths can help us when we encounter the storms that seem to knock our legs out from under us. The wind may be calm and the waves might be manageable, but for certain what is calm now can become a storm later on. No matter who we are, we are certain to experience many storms in life. How will we respond?

Don't look down, don't look back, but look upward toward the heavens, and ask God to give you a new vision and purpose when trials blow into your life. In our family, when the storm crashes in our lives, we ask God this question, "What lesson are You trying to teach us in this experience?"

Without storms in our lives, we can't help others when they experience their own storms. So don't keep this experience to yourself. Be available to help others when their storms hit.

Prayer: Father God, show me Your purpose for each of my storms. Let me learn something so that this trial will serve a purpose for my life. From Scripture and from experience, I know You are always with me. Amen.

Action: In your journal, write about an experience of peace you have had in a storm of your life. Read Paul's prayer in Ephesians 1:18-21.

Today's Wisdom:

It is suffering and then glory. Not to have the suffering means not to have the glory.

—Robert C. McQuilkin

I said, "Sometimes I fail."
He said, "I'll see you through."
I said, "But what if I fall?"
He said, "I will carry you."

I said, "My fears are great!"
He said, "Trust Me alone."
I said, "But I'm depressed."
He said, "I'll cheer you on."

I said, "Life isn't easy."
He said, "Please let Me help.
   Remember, I love you."
I said, "Lord, I accept."

—Perry Tanksley

Be Careful What You Say

The tongue has the power of life and death,
and those who love it will eat its fruit.
—Proverbs 18:21

The tongue is a very powerful tool in our lives. It can bring us death, or it can bring us life. James 1:19-20 gives a very strong warning about this power. It says, "Everyone must be quick to hear, slow to speak and slow to anger; for the anger of man does not achieve the righteousness of God" (NASB).

Words can be used to express our love and admiration for our husbands. We can also communicate with them by how we listen. And often our looks and touches communicate as strongly as our words. These nonverbal signals transmit our feelings in strong fashion. Primarily, though, we need to verbally communicate to our spouses what we are thinking, how we are feeling, what we are dealing with, and what our dreams are. How we transmit these thoughts into words will make a difference in whether our marriages are strong or weak, ones of positivity or negativity, ones of wellness or destruction. One of the key verses that guides us in this area is Ephesians 4:29, "Do not let any unwholesome talk come out of your mouths, but only what is helpful for building others up according to their needs, that it may benefit those who listen."

Since communication is vital to the health of our relationships with our mates, we need to develop the skills necessary for consistent, caring communication. Listening is as valuable as speaking. Good listening creates good bonding. The better we bond, the closer we become. Recognize that communication is an *exchange* of thoughts and ideas. Don't be one who is waiting for a break in your husband's speech so you can jump in and give your speech.

In order to have open communication, be vulnerable and honest, and allow the other person freedom to share without fear, rejection, or negative judgment. When a husband and wife establish a pattern of resolving their differences in a healthy fashion, it permits them to disagree in the future in the same manner.

Once a reporter asked Billy Graham how he and his beloved wife, Ruth, shared intimacy. Billy replied, "We romance with our eyes!" By giving your full attention to your spouse when he is talking, your eyes say, "You're special to me." Rolling your eyes or looking past your spouse at something going on out the window, down the hall, or on the television, however, says, "You are not important to me." Direct your eyes lovingly at him, and show him that everything he says matters.

Prayer: Father God, give me the desire to be a good communicator with my husband. Let me listen before I speak, and let my tongue be quiet until I know all the facts. Let me be attentive as we share ideas and thoughts. Amen.

Action: Be quick to hear, slow to speak, and slow to anger.

Today's Wisdom:

The two most important muscles which operate without the direction of the brain are the heart and the tongue.

—AUTHOR UNKNOWN

We Are Seasoners of Life

You are the salt of the earth.
—MATTHEW 5:13

One of our favorite TV programs over the past years has been *Emeril Live*. Emeril is a charismatic chef from New Orleans who is always talking about seasoning and "kicking it up a notch." When he throws in the seasoning, he gives a very active arm and hand motion as he tosses in the added flavor and utters his now famous expression, "BAM!" He loves extra seasoning. In fact, he seems to think that the hotter the better. Of course his fans in the audience applaud each time Emeril says "BAM!" Not only is this good entertainment, it is good cooking. Everyone knows that food with lots of flavor make the most memorable meals of all.

That's the way it is in the Christian life. If we are bland and have no flavor, no one will want to follow our recipe for life. The New Testament tells us that we are to be the salt and light of the earth. We are to be seasoners and to shed light into darkness. We are to be set apart in life by how we live, how we respond, and whom we give credit to when life is going well or when we face trials. There is a difference between Christ followers and the world. "But we all, with unveiled face, beholding as in a mirror the glory of the Lord, are being transformed into the same image from glory to glory, just as from the Lord, the Spirit" (2 Corinthians 3:18 NASB).

As believers, our faces reflect the spirit of the Lord. Our character is often the only Bible the unbelievers will ever read. Our countenance radiates that there is something different about us. Many times people will ask us, "Are you a Christian?" When we say yes, they will say, "I thought so. You seemed to have a calmness about you!"

Our call is twofold: (1) Stand against moral decay and darkness, (2) Bring light and seasoning to the outside world. Throughout Scripture Jesus shares that we are to be influencers in the world. We read:

- "Jesus again spoke to them, saying, 'I am the Light of the world; he who follows Me will not walk in the darkness, but will have the Light of life'" (John 8:12 NASB).

- "Let your light shine before men in such a way that they may see your good works, and glorify your Father who is in heaven" (Matthew 5:16 NASB).

- "Treat people the same way you want them to treat you, for this is the Law and the Prophets" (Matthew 7:12 NASB).

- "The whole Law is fulfilled in one word, in the statement, 'You shall love your neighbor as yourself'" (Galatians 5:14 NASB).

As seasoners, let's be reminded that one of our main purposes is to love, love, and love. Each time we shed light upon a family member, a neighbor, or a fellow worker, we are sharing God's love with that person. Whenever our lives reflect the love of God, our heavenly Father is glorified (see Matthew 5:16).

Prayer: Father God, thank You for impressing on me the importance of being a seasoner to those whom I come in contact with each day. Continue to remind me that I am the light and salt of the world. Amen.

Action: Each time you pick up the saltshaker to season your food, may you be reminded that you are a seasoner of life.

Today's Wisdom:

The deepest principle in human nature is the craving to be appreciated.

—William James

$\mathcal{N}$ever Alone

All my longings lie open before you, O Lord;
my sighing is not hidden from you.
—Psalm 38:9

$\mathcal{W}$hen you are alone, do you ever feel overcome by loneliness? Alone and loneliness are not the same state of being at all, but when the clock ticks slowly at night and we are wide awake, or during the long stretch of days following a trial, it is easy to mistakenly think that we are alone in the world, or at least alone in our circumstance.

Oh, how Satan loves to move in during our darkest hour and take away all our joy. He seems to wait until we are at our lowest point (usually at night, when our minds become restless and wandering) to whisper in our ears that God has forsaken us and offers no hope. These dark hours are tests for us as believers—we are no longer talking about theories and philosophies of life; we are confronted with the reality of life. Do we really believe what we say we believe?

Sometimes during the night while I sleep, I let out a sigh and Bob inquires if I am okay. I'm usually unaware that a sigh has been uttered. I assure him that I'm okay and that my soul was just talking to God.

Perhaps my sigh is saying, *Lord, in my sickness and distress, my whole life is open before You. I've hidden nothing from You. You even hear my sighs. At times, my words don't seem adequate; all that are left are the groans of my soul. I look forward to what You will reveal next. Your plan is my plan.*

After my journey through cancer, I thank God every day for how He is restoring my health to where it was. I am enjoying a quality of life that I never thought I would have. All that the locusts have eaten has been restored to me and my family (see Joel 2:25). One of the big mysteries of life is why He has restored health to me and not to others. He is the Potter. I just have to trust Him in life and in death.

Please remember that in sickness and in health we should allow our souls to speak to God often. Release those sighs of fear, fatigue, disappointment, and also of hope so that the Potter may turn your heartache into something new. The next time night falls and loneliness emerges, find comfort and rest in His presence. You are never alone.

Prayer: Father God, the tears of my sighs have been evident on my pillow. I'm glad You have collected each and every one of them in Your bottle. Thank You for hearing my faintest sigh. Amen.

Action: Trust God, and give your sighs to Him.

Today's Wisdom:

> Have courage for the great sorrows of life and patience for the small ones; and when you have laboriously accomplished your daily task, go to sleep in peace. God is awake.
>
> —Victor Hugo

Organize Your Stuff

Who can discern his errors?
Forgive my hidden faults.
—PSALM 19:12

$\mathscr{I}$f anyone is inquiring…the stuff in my life and its accumulation is my fault. I'm always looking for that right stuff to complement the interior of our home. We all have stuff. It's almost part of being American. But where does one store the stuff? When we recently moved from Riverside to Newport Beach to be closer to my oncologist, we had a huge sale to get rid of a lot of our stuff. Everyone should move every 10 to 15 years just to get rid of all the stuff that is accumulated over the years.

Organization helps us store our possessions. The possibilities are limited only by our creativity. One of my favorite pieces of furniture is an odd little cabinet I bought for $15 at someone's home many years ago. It's long and low, with doors in front. We use it as a table behind our sofa in the family room, with a small lamp and an antique scale on top—but it also offers wonderful storage space for tablecloths and place mats.

Whenever I visit an antique store or a secondhand shop, I'm on the lookout for these kinds of multipurpose pieces. If you have an empty corner in a guest room, something simple like this makes for a lovely visual piece but is also ideal for extra storage room for blankets, pillows, linens, or even for your guest's belongings.

Even a simple cardboard box can be one of your best organizational tools. Rescue them from the recycle bin (or check with your stationery store) and put them to work in the interest of an organized and attractive work space. My mother-in-law stacked up a few of these boxes, topped them with a wooden oval, threw a colorful cloth over that, placed a cute lamp on top, and she had extra storage in the boxes as well as an attractive end table by her sofa or bed.

With just a little thought and creativity, you can definitely keep everything in its organized place. Even though one of my faults is stuff, at least it's organized stuff.

Prayer: Father God, thanks for giving me the ability and desire to organize my stuff. When I'm organized, I don't feel out of control! Amen.

Action: Spend an hour today organizing some of your stuff. And while you are organizing your things, spend time praying for the nonmaterial blessings in your life like health and beauty and friendships. See the abundance in your life.

Today's Wisdom:

We take care of our health, we lay up money, we make our room tight, and our clothing sufficient; but who provides wisely that he shall not be wanting in the best property of all—friends.

—Ralph Waldo Emerson

The Lord IS

The LORD is...
—Psalm 23:1

*I*n his most beautiful psalm of trust, David pictures the Lord as the great Shepherd who provides for and protects His sheep and as the glorious host who protects and provides abundantly for His guests.

At the beginning of this great Psalm 23 we read, "The LORD is..." That's all we need to know. The Lord IS. He is all we need. We don't need any other. He is the hub of our lives. All else revolves around Him. He is what makes sense out of nonsense—this crazy world.

When my good health was disrupted by cancer, I started each new day with this proclamation, "The Lord is." He is:

- my supporter
- my courage
- my encourager
- my trust
- my salvation
- my purpose

He is my beginning and end and all that falls between. Nothing else matters but Jesus. He is the rock, my foundation. He is the hearer and responder to my prayers. At times I haven't even known how to pray, but I know that the Holy Spirit intercedes for me.

Everything that I have, everything that I am, is credited to Him who has made me. My whole purpose in life only matters as it revolves around my relationship with my Lord. The Lord is everything. He is everything for you, too. Believe that. State that. And live your life by that truth.

Prayer: Father God, may I never forget to call on You in every situation. Thank You for being within the sound of my voice. You are my all. Amen.

Action: Complete: The Lord is _____

_____ .

Today's Wisdom:

If I can stop one Heart from breaking,
I shall not live in vain;
If I can ease one Life the Aching,
Or cool one pain,
Or help one fainting Robin
Unto his Nest again,
I shall not live in vain.

—EMILY DICKINSON

Which God Will You Serve?

I will give thanks to the LORD because of his righteousness
and will sing praise to the name of the LORD Most High.
—PSALM 7:17

As humans, we struggle with who will be our god. Will it be a person, a job, more wealth, a possession, or will it be the almighty God? Idolatry happens when we place our longings for what only God can provide in the hands of a created creature instead of the Creator. When we base our lives on false gods created by mankind, instead of depending on God the Creator, we eventually realize that our lives don't have meaning and are void of fulfillment. The writers of Scripture are quite clear that dependency on a false god will result in loss, pain, and shame (see Isaiah 42:17; 44:9-11). A false god will leave emptiness and disappointment.

Joshua, at the end of his life, gave this decree in Joshua 24:15:

> If it is disagreeable in your sight to serve the LORD, choose for yourselves today whom you will serve: whether the gods which your fathers served which were beyond the River, or the gods of the Amorites in whose land you are living; but as for me and my house, we will serve the LORD (NASB).

Here was a man who stood strong in the midst of his family and stated boldly: You may serve whichever god you wish, but for me and my house, we are going to serve the Lord. We face the same decision today. Which god will we serve?

We need to continually evaluate our lives to see why we do what we do. What is our motivation? Are we trying to please the Creator or the created? If we are honest with ourselves, we can change course and go in another direction. It's important that we let God work in our lives. We need to be as soft as new clay so we can be remolded. If we become hard, we become brittle and fragile. We need to keep our eyes on the Lord, so He can direct our paths.

Prayer: Father God, You are my God. Keep me from worshiping false gods of wealth, status, materialism, or pride. You will stay, but those idols will disappear. Let me focus on Your truth. Amen.

Action: Worship and praise the Creator today.

Today's Wisdom:

To have faith is to believe, to trust, to have confidence in, or to rely on something or someone. Faithfulness describes the quality of someone with unswerving allegiance to an oath or a promise. Our example of faithfulness comes from a God who has kept and is in the process of keeping every promise contained in the Scriptures. We are commanded to "have faith in God," and out of that faith flows our ability to remain faithful to people—to keep the promises we have made as husbands and wives, as children, as parents, and as servants of God.

—Elaine Creasman

*L*ive on Solid Ground

He will be the sure foundation for your times,
a rich store of salvation and wisdom and knowledge;
the fear of the LORD is the key to this treasure.
—ISAIAH 33:6

*R*ecently I received a letter from a dear friend whom we financially support in her ministry. She has expressed over the months that God has been guiding her in new ways but the light to the path isn't clear yet. She sees changes on the horizon and isn't sure of what lies ahead, and her letter is a continuation of her search for new direction. She shares this:

> At this point in my life I am facing changes in many respects, and if I did not know the Lord and if I did not know that He establishes and directs my steps, I could be shaken by some of what I see happening around me (Psalm 37:23; Proverbs 16:9).

> As I was thanking Him just a few days ago for the fact that I know He is the same yesterday, today, and forever (Hebrews 13:8) and that although circumstances and relationships may change, He never changes nor forsakes

me (Hebrews 13:5), He brought a verse to my mind that I have known over the years. Through this verse He has also brought comfort to me for these changing times I am in. The verse is Isaiah 33:6: "He will be the stability of your times" (NASB).

Isn't it a comfort to know truths that confirm His faithfulness to us, and then in addition to realize that He is our stability!

The word *stability* means the strength to stand or endure; firmness; the property of a body that causes it, when disturbed from a condition of equilibrium, to develop forces that restore the original condition.

What a promise! When we may feel shaken, He is firm and stands and endures for us! He is that which will always restore us to a condition of equilibrium, no matter what!

If you are not now in a situation in which changing circumstances are a factor, then you may not appreciate fully what this promise has meant to me in these last days, but you know a time will come when changes will be a factor, and, as I said earlier, then you will want to embrace this truth. It will hold you with hope and confidence in a state of changes!

Thank you again for your faithfulness!

Here is one person who can recall and claim God's mighty Scriptures to see us through difficult times. Even though our stability is shaken in the present, He promises that He will always be the same—never wavering.

Changes are part of life. If not today, then surely tomorrow or the next day. Isn't it wonderful to know that when changes come, we can go to God's Word to find the strength to see us through another situation? Let's not wait for the storm to seek verses that comfort and direct, but let's be prepared when these days appear on the horizon (and they surely will) and have these fantastic truths in our memory bank.

Prayer: Father God, I never know when unstable situations will appear in my life. Let me prepare myself with Your Word that will be an encouragement as I travel through difficult times. Amen.

Action: Read: Psalm 37:23; 42:11; Proverbs 16:9; Hebrews 13:8.

Today's Wisdom:

It is not a disgrace to fail. Failing is one of the greatest arts in the world.

—CHARLES KETTERING

Your Days Are Numbered

Just as man is destined to die once, and after that to face judgment,
so Christ was sacrificed once to take away the sins of many people.
—HEBREWS 9:27

If we just had one year to live, what would we do? This is a great question and one that we should think through. In fact many of us will not have the luxury of living one year after we are told we have a terminal illness or if we suffer a sudden death by natural causes.

A.W. Tozer wrote a response to this basic question of life. See if your thoughts might be similar to his:

> I would put away apathy, come boldly to Christ, and throw myself at His feet: "Believe on the Lord Jesus Christ, and thou shalt be saved."…I would come believing that God's promise of forgiveness and eternal life includes me.

> Then, a new person in Christ, I would give the last remaining year to God. All the wreckage and loss of the years behind me would spur me on to make the one year before me a God-blessed success.

Now all this would seem to me to be the good and right thing to do for one who had just a year to live. But since we do not know whether we have a year before us, or a day or 10 days, and since what would be right for the last year would be right for the whole life—even if its years were many—then the conclusion is plain. Our cry to God should be, "Teach us to number our days, that we may apply our hearts to wisdom" (Psalm 90:12).[19]

Where would your current beliefs lead you if you faced this scenario? Are you strong in the Lord? Or have you depended too much on your own strength and ability for so long that you have distanced yourself from complete dependence on God? If your days are limited (and let's face it...they are), could you begin to lean on the Lord for everything—direction, hope, dreams, faith, contentment, fulfillment, protection, security?

Would you share your understanding of Christ's grace and forgiveness with others? Would you live out your faith with excitement, generosity, and the hope of eternal life?

Take time to consider how you'd change if you had only 365 days before you died, then consider how much your life will change because you know you'll live forever with the Lord!

Prayer: Father God, teach me to number my days and to live each day, week, month, and year as if it were my last. May I reconfirm my purpose in life. Let me not waste my time serving just myself. Challenge me today in a new way. Amen.

Action: Write in your journal what you would do if you had just one year to live. Discuss this with your mate.

Today's Wisdom:

Saying "Yes!" to God is not a simple matter because making our lives into lives of love is not a simple or easy thing. To choose love as a life principle means that my basic mind-set or question must be: What is the loving thing to be, to do, to say? My consistent response to each of life's events, to each person who enters and touches my life, to each demand on my time and nerves and heart, must somehow be transformed into an act of love. However, in the last analysis, it is this "Yes!" that opens me to God. Choosing love as a life principle widens the chalice of my soul, so that God can pour into me His gifts and graces and powers.

—JOHN POWELL

Discovering Your Story

You have a story to tell. You might not realize it because you don't have an immediate reason to tell it or write it. But you have a story. Someday it may come out. For years, I have shared some of my story in order to encourage women I meet. Whether I am speaking at a conference or having tea with a group of ladies from church, I like to engage in the exchange of personal stories. We discover so much about God's goodness and grace when we know how He has moved in another's life.

Because I dedicated this book to my friend Florence Littauer, I wanted to share with you my personal story and my initial connection with her. Her influence came at such an important time in my life and in my spiritual journey as well.

When I was a new empty nester; the two children were away to college and my purpose in life had been fulfilled (at least I thought so). I got down on my knees beside my bed one morning and cried out to God to show me what I was to do for the rest of my life. I said, "God, if You can use me I'm at Your service. I have no formal education, I have no working skills. I've been a homemaker for the last eighteen years; that's all I know. Use me any way You can. I'm Yours."

At the same time I had become acquainted with a prominent Christian writer and speaker (yes, this was Florence!), and after a couple of years of friendship, she suggested that I might consider writing a book. I was dumbfounded. I didn't know how to write. Yes, I had spoken before large audiences about my Christian faith—with good response. But a writer? I had no confidence in that area.

Shortly after that conversation with Florence, I received a phone call from her publishing company. Of course, I had no book to offer, but after the president and I had a great conversation, he asked me to send him any tapes, outlines, and written materials pertaining to my area of expertise—home organization. I was happy to comply, but not very confident that anything would happen.

Weeks later, I received a package containing a manuscript transcribed from my materials. That manuscript became my very first book, *More Hours in My Day,* and was the beginning of a wonderful ministry that has brought God's Word and principles to hundreds of thousands of readers. What I thought was insignificant, God knew would be built up to serve Him. Each day I am thankful for all those who encouraged me along the journey.

God heard me when I asked for direction and a way to be used by Him. Use your story to tell others of God's faithfulness and mercy. You need not write books or have a ministry to countless others. The telling of your story is the telling of God's love, and it is a way to praise His name. Most important, place the unfolding story of your life in His hands and get ready to share it!

Prayer: Father God, I appreciate the confidence You have in me. Give me a sense of the vision You have for my life. May I walk with faithfulness each day in that way. Amen.

Action: Give your personal story some thought. Begin to

share it, write it, pray about it, and lift it up to God.

Today's Wisdom:

I am only one,
But still I am one.
I cannot do everything,
But still I can do something;
And because I cannot do everything
I will not refuse to do something
that I can do.

—EDWARD EVERETT HALE

$\mathscr{N}$otes

1. The Tract League, Grand Rapids, MI, Tract #185.

2. Robert J. Morgan, *Then Sings My Soul* (Nashville: Nelson, 2003), p. 261.

3. Joe Gatuslao, *Good News Journal* #4, no. 1 (2002): p. 18.

4. Elaine Wright Colvin and Elaine Creasman, *Treasury of God's Virtues* (Lincoln-wood, IL: Publications International, 1999), p. 246.

5. Colvin and Creasman, p. 112.

6. www.helensteinerrice.com

7. Charles C. Ryrie, *Ryrie Study Bible, New American Standard* (Chicago: Moody, 1978), p. 1568, Luke 11:13 footnote.

8. Rick Warren, *The Purpose-Driven Life* (Grand Rapids, MI: Zondervan, 2002), p. 7.

9. Bob and Emilie Barnes, adapted from *15 Minute Devotions for Couples* (Eugene, OR: Harvest House, 1995), pp. 169-73.

10. Emilie Barnes, adapted from *Minute Meditations for Women* (Eugene, OR: Harvest House, 1999), p. 214.

11. Emilie Barnes, adapted from *More Faith in My Day* (Eugene, OR: Harvest House, 2005), pp. 183-84.

12. Lee Iacocca, *Talking Straight* (New York: Bantam Books, 1988), p. 27.

13. George Beverly Shea/Rhea F. Miller, "I'd Rather Have Jesus" (Waco, TX: Word Music), 1939.

14. Ray Stedman, *Reason to Rejoice* (Grand Rapids, MI: Discovery House, 2004), pp. 243-45.

15. Author unknown.

16. Larry Crabb, *The Marriage Builder* (Grand Rapids, MI: Zondervan, 1982), pp. 105-6.

17. Author unknown—e-mail.

18. Beth Wohlford, ed., Women's Ministry bulletin, Willow Creek Community Church, Barrington, IL, Sunday, August 27, 1995.

19. American Tract Society, Garland, TX.

Other Harvest House Books
by Emilie Barnes

The 15-Minute Organizer

15 Minutes Alone with God

15 Minutes of Peace
with God

15 Minutes with God
for Grandma

101 Ways to Lift Your Spirits

Cleaning Up the Clutter

A Cup of Hope

Emilie's Creative
Home Organizer

Everything I Know
I Learned in My Garden

Everything I Know
I Learned over Tea

Friendship Teas to Go

A Grandma
Is a Gift from God

Heal My Heart, Lord

Home Warming

I Need Your Strength, Lord

If Teacups Could Talk

An Invitation to Tea

Join Me for Tea

Keep It Simple
for Busy Women

Let's Have a Tea Party!

A Little Book of Manners

Minute Meditations
for Busy Moms

Minute Meditations for Healing
and Hope

Minute Meditations
for Women

More Faith in My Day

More Hours in My Day

Quiet Moments for
a Busy Mom's Soul

A Quiet Refuge

Safe in the Father's Hands

Simple Secrets to
a Beautiful Home

Strength for Today,
Bright Hope for Tomorrow

A Tea to Comfort Your Soul

The Twelve Teas®
of Celebration

The Twelve Teas®
of Christmas

The Twelve Teas®
of Friendship

Other Great Harvest House Reading

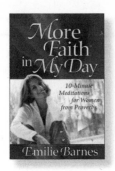

MORE FAITH IN MY DAY
10-Minute Meditations for Women from Proverbs

Emilie invites you to take a moment away from daily demands to rejuvenate your heart and mind with wisdom from Proverbs. *More Faith in My Day* offers the Bible's insights to your heart through features like...

- devotions inspired by Proverbs' teachings of goodness, love, work, family
- "Today's Wisdom" to enrich personal faith life
- ideas to turn God's abundant knowledge into action
- prayers for moments of meditation and connection

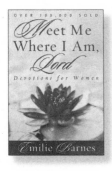

MEET ME WHERE I AM, LORD
Devotions for Women

In these short but thought-provoking meditations created especially for busy women, you can experience the lasting refreshment of God's presence meeting you...right where you are. Emilie Barnes offers...

- devotions to inspire and encourage
- practical suggestions for infusing life with faith
- closing prayers to place concerns in God's hands
- Bible verses for wisdom and comfort
- space to write reflections

A QUIET REFUGE
Prayers and Meditations for Hope and Healing

This selection of prayers and meditations offers you stepping-stones to a personal sanctuary. You'll discover restoration and hope in Kathleen Denis's paintings of inviting gardens, beckoning beachside chairs, and welcoming, sheltered spaces. Perfect for giving as a gift and for keeping within heart's reach, this collection offers you renewal for the journey and a quiet place to feel God's presence.

To learn more about books by Emilie Barnes
or to read sample chapters, log on to our website:
www.harvesthousepublishers.com

HARVEST HOUSE PUBLISHERS
EUGENE, OREGON